Athlone French Poets

GUILLAUME APOLLINAIRE

Athlone French Poets

General Editor EILEEN LE BRETON

*Reader in French Language and Literature,
Bedford College, University of London*

Monographs

GERARD DE NERVAL

THEOPHILE GAUTIER

VERLAINE

JULES LAFORGUE

GUILLAUME APOLLINAIRE

SAINT-JOHN PERSE

Critical Editions

VICTOR HUGO : CHATIMENTS

GERARD DE NERVAL : LES CHIMERES

ALFRED DE MUSSET : CONTES D'ESPAGNE ET D'ITALIE

THEOPHILE GAUTIER : POESIES

PAUL VERLAINE : SAGESSE

PAUL VERLAINE : ROMANCES SANS PAROLES

ARTHUR RIMBAUD : LES ILLUMINATIONS

JULES LAFORGUE : LES COMPLAINTES

PAUL VALERY : CHARMES OU POEMES

GUILLAUME APOLLINAIRE : ALCOOLS

SAINT-JOHN PERSE : EXIL

Guillaume Apollinaire

by

ROGER LITTLE

UNIVERSITY OF LONDON
THE ATHLONE PRESS
1976

Published by
THE ATHLONE PRESS
UNIVERSITY OF LONDON
at 4 Gower Street, London WC1

Distributed by
Tiptree Book Services Ltd
Tiptree, Essex

U.S.A. and Canada
Humanities Press Inc
New Jersey

© *Roger Little* 1976

0 485 14608 8 *cloth*
0 485 12208 1 *paperback*

Printed in Great Britain by
The Garden City Press Limited
Letchworth, Hertfordshire
SG6 1JS

Athlone French Poets

General Editor EILEEN LE BRETON

This series is designed to provide students and general readers both with Monographs on important nineteenth- and twentieth-century French poets and Critical Editions of one or more representative works by these poets.

The Monographs aim at presenting the essential biographical facts while placing the poet in his social and intellectual context. They contain a detailed analysis of his poetical works and, where appropriate, a brief account of his other writings. His literary reputation is examined and his contribution to the development of French poetry is assessed, as is also his impact on other literatures. A selection of critical views and a bibliography are appended.

The critical Editions contain a substantial introduction aimed at presenting each work against its historical background as well as studying its genre, structure, themes, style, etc. and highlighting its relevance for today. The text normally given is the complete text of the original edition. It is followed by full commentaries on the poems and annotation of the text, including variant readings when these are of real significance.

E. Le B.

PREFACE

Apollinaire appears to lend himself to the 'critical biography' approach. It has long seemed to me, however, that the man was often made to get in the way of his poetry in more or less critical attempts to justify it. My aim in writing this book has therefore been an exploratory as well as an explanatory one. Without rejecting any facts obtained by biographers or literary historians, I have tried to see to what extent an aesthetic approach can usefully complement their findings and so, in particular, how steadily the poetry can stand on its own feet.

So much is available on Apollinaire, even in English, that I felt free to take an interpretative line even within the compass of a series meant primarily to be informative. The admirable pioneering work by Pierre-Marcel Adéma and Michel Décaudin, the sensitive criticism of Marie-Jeanne Durry, Margaret Davies, Philippe Renaud, Jean-Claude Chevalier and others, all that and more forms a backdrop to any interpretation of Apollinaire's poetry. He seems rather like a public speaker who 'needs no introduction'. Continuing to attract young people, he generates fresh evaluations. I have tried to analyse both his appeal and his limitations, and where I present personal opinions hope to contribute to the continuing debate. Where other readers disagree with me (and I expect no less), I trust my suggestions will sharpen Occam's razor so that a clean cut may be made in them.

Since Apollinaire, poetry has not been the same. But *post hoc* and *propter hoc* require careful distinction when a man is so bound up with an artistic and social revolution as Apollinaire was with the aesthetic experiments and traumatic experiences of the early years of this century. To guide me towards my conclusions I have relied principally on Apollinaire's own writings. I am all the more grateful to the Inter-University Council for Higher Education Overseas for a special grant to buy the *Œuvres complètes*: it enabled me to continue preparing this monograph while attached to the University of Sierra Leone. Pierre Oster Soussouev kindly traced a copy of the now rare volumes for me.

Professor C. A. Hackett and Louis Allen, most welcome visitors to West Africa, gave up precious time to read part of the typescript and make valuable suggestions. Michael Sheringham and Michael Bishop responded to my pleas for photocopies of material by Breton and Reverdy I needed. Dr Eileen Le Breton, as general editor of the series, moderated my text with thorough-going wisdom and drew my attention to recent publications which had escaped me. I am most grateful to all of them for their help. And to my wife, whose keen critical eye followed every stage of preparation, my thanks go beyond words.

In my tropical fastness, writing this book, I often recalled Apollinaire's words and took some ironic comfort from them:

On se défie trop en France des goûts de l'étranger. Ils pourraient au moins servir d'indication. On devrait, ce semble, considérer que l'étranger, placé en dehors des côteries parisiennes, en dehors de l'influence d'une critique souvent esclave et rarement désintéressée, va naturellement aux efforts les plus importants, aux œuvres dont la beauté lui paraît la plus nouvelle et la moins discutable. (*O.C.*, iv, 87)

R. L.

CONTENTS

For my students at Fourah Bay College,
who made it all worthwhile

I

KOSTRO

Mystification about one's private life may be either self-indulgence or a form of reticence. Characteristically, in Apollinaire's complex personality, it was both. His attitude towards his own origins, which really needed no romantic embroidering to capture interest, was typical in this respect. Hints and half-truths were woven into a legend by friends and acquaintances prepared to flatter his taste for self-dramatisation and respect his deep-seated need for privacy. Now he was the product of the Pope's fleshly lapse; now directly descended from Napoleon through l'Aiglon. Rome was certainly his birthplace, an unmarried Polish girl, Angeliska Kostrowicka, indubitably his mother; the rest was largely conjecture until the patient detective work of critics, notably Pierre-Marcel Adéma, pieced together sufficient facts for a reasonably full, authenticated picture to emerge over thirty years after the poet's death. In 'A une raison' in his *Illuminations*, Rimbaud declares: 'Arrivée de toujours, qui t'en iras partout'. It is as if Apollinaire wanted to apply the idea to himself as archetypal poet of the magus variety. Much of his writing stems from a sometimes desperate attempt to acquire the culture of his adopted country so as to find a firm platform for the kind of universality that disparate eclecticism cannot provide.

Seemingly addressing himself in 'Le Larron' in *Alcools*, Apollinaire writes:

> Maraudeur étranger malheureux malhabile
>
> ...
>
> Ton père fut un sphinx et ta mère une nuit

But what are the facts? He was born in the Italian capital in late August 1880, probably the 26th, the illegitimate son of an impulsive girl of aristocratic Polish stock who found herself at the Vatican because of her father's grace and favour position there. After some initial hesitations, the child was registered under the name Guglielmo Alberto Wladimiro Apollinare de

Kostrowitzky, and Guillaume Kostrowitzky, with or without the
particle which his mother had assumed, remained his official
name. His father's identity long remained a riddle, but Adéma's
well-documented hypothesis that he was Francesco Flugi
d'Aspermont, of patrician Piedmontese descent, is now generally
accepted.[1] After a second boy was born of the same illicit union,
the father left his mistress who sought consolation in the casinos
of the French Riviera where she settled with her children.
Guillaume's school years, when he acquired the nickname
Kostro, were first spent in Monaco at the Roman Catholic
Collège Saint-Charles where he made his solemn first commun-
ion in 1892 and stayed until it closed down in 1896. The next
academic session was shared between the Collège Stanislas at
Cannes and the lycée at Nice in a vain attempt to pass his
baccalauréat. His winning if wayward personality and his exten-
sive if erratic reading sealed a number of lasting friendships
(with René Dalize and Toussaint Luca for instance) and certainly impressed his schoolmates. Kostro was already an enchan-
ter. His capacity to remember out-of-the-way details and anecdotal incidents made him a charming raconteur, and if this
required no particular originality on his part it did make him
excellent company. In his published stories we shall find both the
same appeal and the same lack of originality.

1899 brought some notable incidents. Miss Kostrowitzky, now
teamed up with Jules Weil, a not-too-successful financier who
was to remain her companion to the end, moved to Paris with
her sons whom she promptly installed at Stavelot in Belgium for
the summer holidays while she was trying to sort out her
financial difficulties and consolidate her position. Stavelot not
only saw Apollinaire's first love poems, addressed to Maria (or
'Mareye') Dubois of the local café, but also an incident which
had considerable repercussions: his mother wrote to the boys
giving them orders to leave their boarding-house without paying
the bill. The reason was simply lack of money, and Kostro was to
have to face this fact for the first time in his life. It undermined
his already somewhat precarious sense of security, and even
when recounting the incident and its aftermath three years later
to a friend, with a strict injunction not to divulge the contents of

his letter, a painful feeling of almost breathless desperation is
conveyed:

Départ à la cloche de bois par un temps de gel, la nuit, avec malle sur le
dos valise à la main à travers 7 kilom. de forêt, odeur de champignons
de Stavelot à Roanne Coo heureusement pas de rencontre. 2 h. dans le
froid devant la gare de Roanne Coo et départ pour Paris. A la frontière
Erquelines, le commissaire veut m'arrêter parce que mon nom ressemble à celui d'un anarcho, croyant qu'il m'en veut à cause de la
cloche de bois je me trouble. Enfin il reconnaît son erreur et me laisse
refiler avec mon frère. Ma mère était à Paris. A Paris hiver difficile. On
arrive à croire qu'on mangera des briques... Je traîne sans place.
(*O.C.*, iv, 714)

As an unqualified foreigner, Kostro found it impossible for two
years to obtain secure employment and while doing odd jobs in
finance and 'ghosting' for a hack story-writer, he pursued his
overriding interest in poetry and literature. He had plans for a
play, wrote a novel and promptly lost the manuscript, and
dedicated some poems to his latest girl-friend, Linda Molina.
When the opportunity to act as private tutor to the daughter of
the Countess of Milhau in Germany presented itself, Kostro did
not hesitate to accept.

For a year from August 1901, Kostro was based in the
Rhineland. It was a period of intense literary activity inspired
partly by the Rhine itself with its romantic literary associations
and partly by the English governess, Annie Playden, also employed in the Milhau household. *La Revue blanche* published a
story signed Guillaume Apollinaire and poems were written now
which were to figure importantly in *Alcools* over ten years later.
Annie Playden, the pretty, strait-laced girl from Landor Road in
Clapham, aroused her colleague's Slavonic-Latin ardour and
even, if we are to believe Kostro's somewhat boastful confession
both to a friend and to a later girl-friend, allowed him some
physical favours. 'L'Anglaise ... était épatante, blonde comme la
lune, des tétons épatants, gros et fermes et droits, qui bandaient
dès qu'on les touchait et la mettaient de suite en chaleur, un cul
mirobolant énorme et une taille mince à ravir' (*Lettres à Lou*, p.
103). Yet it was her very reluctance to accept his advances that
most stimulated his poetic vein. His passionate desire to make of
love a master-slave relationship both in the satisfaction of his

colourfully varied physical demands and in the unquestioning obedience of his partner was to create problems in all his affairs of the heart. Given the reciprocal nature of love, a complaint of being 'mal aimé' is tantamount to a confession of 'aimer mal'. Guillaume Apollinaire was born: Kostro's loss was poetry's gain, yet another example of the abiding ironic adage, formulated by Robert Graves, that a poet cannot marry his Muse. Even a year, even two years after returning to Paris from Germany, Apollinaire felt so ardently towards Annie that he went twice to London to seek her out and ask for her hand. The suit was rejected. More frightened than flattered, Annie left for the United States, free from a passion she could not comprehend, free from the biographical anecdote hunters until nearly the end of her modest life, and blissfully unaware of how Apollinaire had celebrated her refusal of him in one of his most important poems, 'La Chanson du mal-aimé'.

Meantime, still failing to find satisfactory employment but making a meagre living in banking and the stock exchange, Apollinaire involved himself more and more with the journalistic and literary scene, attending gatherings and making the acquaintance of various writers including Alfred Jarry whose spirit was to preside over *Les Mamelles de Tirésias*. Constantly on the hunt for publishers for his writings as were others of his young literary friends such as André Salmon, Apollinaire suggested a solution he was to use several times, namely to create his own outlet. In November 1903 appeared the first number of the little magazine *Le Festin d'Esope*, with Apollinaire as editor and first contributor. His tale *L'Enchanteur pourrissant* was first published in instalments in it in 1904, and it was to have nine issues before disappearing. In 1905, a further magazine was financed for Apollinaire. It had two issues and two titles, *La Revue immoraliste* and *Les Lettres modernes*, before going the way of most little magazines. But Apollinaire's range of friends had broadened, and as well as knowing writers including, from 1904, Max Jacob, he had taken a step which was to reveal a whole new world to him, one which he would explore with his customary passion and which would have profound repercussions on his life and work: the world of painting. In 1904, he met Picasso who, with Braque two or three years later, was to trigger off the movement which, according to Apollinaire, Matisse disparagingly christened cubism. Ignorant but fascinated, Apollinaire became increasingly involved with art and artists. The relatively unproductive years 1904–7 were to give way to a new flurry of activity and publication.

The new spate of excitement over people and what they were doing was typical of Apollinaire's enthusiasm but also characteristic of a lack of reasoned discrimination. Uncomprehending at first and generally antipathetic to their work, he came to defend his new friends initially out of a sense of loyalty to them as friends and the constant need to find material for his columns. Gradually he became drawn further and further in, though never acquiring total commitment to a single style or school. It was almost in spite of himself therefore that he became one of the earliest and most influential champions of cubism and through his new-found involvement with art came to meet the gay and capricious painter who was to be his close companion for six years, from 1907 to 1913: Marie Laurencin. So infatuated with her was he that he even moved house to be nearer her. Inevitably he overrated her work, often ranking her with Picasso, but there was in any case an unavoidable tendency for someone so much more bound up with the immediacy of relationships with people than with patient analysis to allow friendship to colour his judgement. His volatile temperament and range of interests made him lively company, and this period of his life was rich in social and literary gatherings at cafés which are remembered as part of the legend of a carefree Paris in the *belle époque.*

Apollinaire both contributed to and derived some reflected benefit from the excitement of the period. It was one of remarkable discoveries and developments. Faith in science as a vector of progress was still very much alive and the popular imagination caught by the spread of new applications: automobiles, wireless, aeroplanes and so on. Communications received a special boost. The arts responded to and helped generate further this euphoric exhilaration: Debussy and Stravinsky in music, Diaghilev in ballet, Antoine in the theatre, Picasso, Braque and a dozen others in painting. Paris was cosmopolitan and extravert, and Apollinaire bore its torch for poetry. Yet behind the *insouciance* and the attitudinising, behind the brittle gaiety, behind the easy generalisations lay, for Apollinaire at least, the regular toil to make ends meet and allow him to indulge, both literally and metaphorically, his wanton, omnivorous appetite. Edging his way ever more firmly into journalism, but not hesitating to publish licentious novels to boost his income, he became the accredited critic of *L'Intransigeant* and editor of two series of books of the type generally sold under plain cover. His serious interest in licentious literature was symptomatic of his love of byways and he indulged it in various ways, by presenting works little-known at the time (including Sade), by writing erotic fantasies himself, and by compiling with a friend an analytical catalogue of the holdings in the 'Enfer' of the Bibliothèque Nationale.

1910 saw the appearance of a collection of his short stories under the title *L'Hérésiarque et Cie*, a contender for the Prix Goncourt. The next year came a collection of short poems illustrated by Raoul Dufy, *Le Bestiaire ou Cortège d'Orphée* and a regular column in *Le Mercure de France* entirely in Apollinaire's inconsequential, random vein: 'La Vie anecdotique'. But his increasing material security was not proof against his arrest and imprisonment on a charge of being involved with the theft of Leonardo da Vinci's 'Mona Lisa' from the Louvre. His acquaintance with a dubious Belgian adventurer Géry Piéret, whose wealth of outlandish experiences captivated Apollinaire's imagination but who, as it turned out, was innocent of the crime, brought him in September 1911 six days' imprisonment in La Santé: in French law there is no *habeas corpus*, and you are guilty until proved innocent. Apollinaire's detractors found it simple justice that a pornographer—and an alien one at that—should be brought to book. His reputation as a *fumiste* did not help: reviewing non-existent books and adopting pseudonyms (including a feminine one) may be innocence or contempt, but are not designed to placate critics or jealous rivals. Even some close friends deserted and denied him. The fragile nature of his status was again brought forcibly home to him: at any moment until his name was finally cleared in January 1912 he could expect expulsion. The Paris he so loved and sang, the French whose life and culture he had devoted so much time to assimilating, the

French language he had explored in its dialects and archaisms, in its beauties and obscurities, all this counted for nothing in the dock.

At the instigation of André Billy, and partly to boost Apollinaire's morale, a small group of friends launched *Les Soirées de Paris*, a monthly magazine which survived from early 1912 until the outbreak of war thanks to an injection of capital at one stage by Serge Férat and his sister. But the event which probably affected Apollinaire most deeply in 1912, and certainly the one which left the most direct traces in his poetry was the ending of his affair with Marie Laurencin. The break came in the autumn, 'ma saison mentale' as Apollinaire calls it, in recognition of his melancholic moods. Three years later he was to write less sentimentally: 'Marie L. ravissamment faite, un des plus gros derrières du monde et que je transperçais avec un âcre plaisir. Elle n'est pas plus que du crottin' (*Lettres à Lou*, p. 103). He felt he could no longer live in Auteuil near the Pont Mirabeau and moved to a flat in the Boulevard Saint-Germain which was to be his final base.

Two notable books appeared in the spring of 1913, both of them collections of earlier, mostly published, writings. The first was *Méditations esthétiques: Les Peintres cubistes*, the second *Alcools: Poèmes 1898–1913*, and they are understandably not without their affinities in spite of their obvious differences. If variety became in them a kind of aesthetic principle in addition to a conscious building of the new on the old, we should not perhaps be too taken aback that Apollinaire's next publication, in June, was a Futurist squib, *L'Antitradition futuriste*, in which he recklessly called for the suppression, among other things, of 'la douleur poétique', 'l'adjectif', 'maisons' etc. Apollinaire's open-mindedness was admirable up to a point but bespoke a void at the centre which fitted him for the gossip-column but never allowed the formulation of a coherent aesthetic attitude. In a letter he confided: 'C'est chez moi raisonnement et instinct et même l'instinct vient avant: c'est peut-être ma seule qualité d'ailleurs' (*Lettres à Lou*, p. 170). His readiness to follow his instinct to experiment led him, in 1913, to launch into a fascinating byway linking verbal and visual forms, his 'idéogrammes lyriques' or 'calligrammes'.

When war threatened in the summer of 1914 and Frenchmen were mobilised, Apollinaire was on a journalistic assignment with André Rouveyre at Deauville. His livelihood was as much in jeopardy as Paris appeared to be, so he left for Nice to join several of his friends. There, in a haze of cocaine, he had a short-lived but passionately sensual affair with 'Lou', Madame Louise de Coligny-Châtillon, whose rejection of him, combined with lack of work and money, led him to enlist in an artillery regiment at Nîmes. As a foreigner, he was not obliged to join up, but doubtless he felt both a sense of patriotism for his adopted country and some unease at knowing all his French friends to be at the front. But given his volatile nature he is at least as likely to have enlisted out of pique at Lou's rebuff as through inner persuasion.

Once enrolled, however, Apollinaire is in his element. Training to be an officer, he is given a horse and a batman and thoroughly relishes the discipline and the panache. Jingoism seems to suit him as well as his colourful uniform. In the early stages he treats the whole thing with his usual sense of dramatic self-involvement, of uncritical make-believe: 'il me semble que le métier de soldat était mon vrai métier. J'aime beaucoup ça. Mon amie [i.e. Lou] prétend que je suis sans cesse à l'opéra, et c'est vrai' (*O.C.*, iv, 781). Once he had a taste for martial derring-do, he was impatient to go to the front, but again not a considered attitude but a final failure at reconciliation with Lou on his terms was the direct cause of his request to go, abandoning his officer-training to depart as a simple gunner. Once at the front, he found the necessary excitement to make him forget the tedium of the training camp: 'La guerre est décidément une fort belle chose et malgré tous les risques que je cours, les fatigues, le manque absolu d'eau et en somme de tout, ... je ne suis pas mécontent du tout d'y être venu' (*O.C.*, iv, 749). One of the things he most lacked was female company; so while continuing to write as a friend to Lou he started in May 1915 an intense correspondence with a girl he had met on a train that January. The girl was Madeleine Pagès who came from Oran, Algeria, and their epistolary relationship led to their engagement in August: such was the power of Apollinaire's charm! But the two were to meet only once again before Apollinaire's flexible capacity for passionate involvement had espoused another cause.

For the time being, all Apollinaire's virility went towards being a good gunner: 'Je fais ce que je peux pour être un parfait militaire' (*O.C.*, iv, 732). He nonetheless found time to publish in the camp at the front a limited hand-copied edition of 'Case d'armons' which would later form a section of the volume *Calligrammes*. Quickly winning promotion, he remained ambitious to become an officer and did so by the simple means of transferring to a less technical branch of the army, the infantry. He became a second lieutenant, but it was his only gain. His innocent delight at playing soldiers, his ingenuous statements like 'La guerre est une chose charmante' (*O.C.*, iv, 917) disappeared in the face of actual warfare, the mud and misery of the front-line trenches. Suddenly he found himself faced with the reality of a static war that was to claim some ten million lives.

Indirectly, it also cost Apollinaire his own life and certainly made a very different man of him according to all his friends and acquaintances. For on 17 March 1916, only eight days after his year-old request to be naturalised French had been granted, a shell fragment pierced his helmet and lodged in his right temple. After a preliminary operation he was evacuated out of the war zone and transferred in the end to the Italian Hospital in Paris where his friend Serge Férat was acting as a nurse. His new collection of short stories, *Le Poète assassiné*, whose title held an ironic grain of truth, appeared at the same time as he was suffering from fainting fits and partial paralysis. The doctors agreed he would have to be trepanned, a delicate operation consisting of drilling a hole in the skull to remove, in this case, an abscess caused by a tiny splinter of shell. From now on his original army medical report—'constitution très bonne, tempérament nerveux' (*O.C.*, iv, 814)—was true in the second respect alone.

He used his protracted convalescence to renew his contacts with the literary and journalistic world, a less lively but no less portly figure on the Paris scene, pleased with the extra attention and sympathy his bandaged head elicited. In his honour a banquet was given at which it was more than apparent that he was considered one of the leaders of the *avant-garde* movement. In Pierre Albert-Birot's magazine *Sic* he declared that the cinema would be the popular art form of the future; he wrote in Picabia's *391* and Reverdy's *Nord-Sud*, both periodicals in the vanguard of fashion; he coined the word 'surréaliste' and wrote *Les Mamelles de Tirésias*, a farce with a moral in the *Ubu* tradition. Yet in 1917 too he published a slender volume of elegantly turned quatrains thereby asserting no less his links with the past. And all the while, not having been discharged from the army, his daily routine work was, ironically enough, in the head office of press censorship. Towards the end of 1917 he gave an important lecture on 'L'Esprit nouveau et les poètes' in which he posited surprise as a new aesthetic principle and quoted from a variety of poets, including himself, who in his view 'laissent deviner un effort indépendant vers l'esprit nouveau' (*O.C.*, iii, 935).

Ill health marked the beginning of 1918 which was an eventful year in many respects. In March, *Calligrammes* was published with the sub-title *Poèmes de la paix et de la guerre (1913–1916)*. In May he married Jacqueline Kolb, 'la jolie rousse', in a last search for a stable relationship, and undertook fresh assignments with newspapers to help pay for their extra needs. In the spring he completed a play of mediocre quality, *Couleur du temps*, and in the summer an *opéra bouffe* libretto, *Casanova*, of no greater interest. Even if his work for the army was minimal, he was overtaxing his strength, and after further bouts of ill-health in the autumn he fell prey to the epidemic of Spanish influenza which gripped the world and indeed killed even more people than the war did. On 9 November 1918, aged 38, Apollinaire died. In the streets outside people shouted 'A bas Guillaume!' but not at Kostro: at Kaiser Wilhelm whose Germany declared itself a republic that very day in readiness for the armistice to be signed two days later. The fatuous struggle and the futile suffering were over.

It is hardly surprising that so prolific and unsystematic a writer should have more posthumous volumes to his name than the meagre few printed during his lifetime. Poems, letters and articles have been patiently assembled and in some cases deciphered by critics and admirers, and there is still material to be revealed including such correspondence as there was with Picasso and Marie Laurencin. Some items are so scurrilous that they cannot yet be printed, but adventurous publishers have of late felt able to offer, for example, a new edition of *Les Onze Mille Verges*, a book that Apollinaire himself kept in a brown paper wrapper. For present purposes, reference is generally made to the only existing edition of the *Œuvres complètes*, any departures from this being indicated where appropriate. For poems from *Alcools* and *Calligrammes*, however, since these exist in various accessible editions, the titles alone are given.

The sheer variety of Apollinaire's output is a measure of his shifting but always whole-hearted enthusiasms. His own life, as we have seen, had all the colours of a chameleon and he drew both on his own direct experience and on the accounts of a wide social spectrum of friends and acquaintances for his literary and journalistic work. We must beware of approving the poetry just because we are intrigued by the man. The close relationship of his biography to his writing has led most critics to adopt a biographical approach, but therein lies a danger of falling prey to the fallacy of judging the work by the spurious criterion of its 'sincerity'. With Apollinaire more than with many writers it is essential to bear in mind the axiom spelt out by Wellek and Warren in their *Theory of Literature*: 'No biographical evidence can change or influence critical evaluation.'[2] In literature, to re-apply Rimbaud's terse phrase, '*Je* est un autre'. Kostro both is and is not Guillaume Apollinaire.

II

'ALCOOLS'

Protesting against a charge of unoriginality brought against *Alcools* by a caustic reviewer, Apollinaire wrote in a letter: 'Je crois n'avoir point imité, car chacun de mes poèmes est la commémoration d'un événement de ma vie' (*O.C.*, iv, 768). This disingenuous protest is double-edged: in seeking to exonerate himself on one relatively minor count, he exposes himself to a second more serious charge of writing private poetry, poetry that is so bound up with his autobiography that it fails to communicate. His claim furthermore afforded apparent justification to well-meaning critics who proposed partial biographical 'explanations' of the poems instead of real analyses and evaluations. Many, of course, shed light and had valuable insights and observations; their work should not be neglected for the sake of any fashionable partisan approach. But it would seem essential, once we have taken advantage of all the relevant facts, to judge whether the work stands on its own feet. We must not confuse the known facts of the poet's existence with the Protean life of his imagination. The superficial reader may believe he has grasped the poetry because he knows the man's external biography: communication then appears simplicity itself. But this, of course, is a delusion: there can never be such an easy one-to-one relationship between biography and the written word. Our attention will therefore be trained on the linguistic phenomena through which the poet reaches towards his reader: they are more intimately revealing than any laundry-bills.

The sub-title of *Alcools*, namely *Poèmes 1898–1913*, situates the collection not only in the *belle époque* but also at a particular stage of Apollinaire's life, from late adolescence to early manhood. Yet there is a conscious rejection of any chronological approach in the ordering of the poems. Apollinaire makes no attempt to guide us through his wayward life and loves or psychological development. Rather does he present a selection of snapshots, some of them decidedly faded, which evoke almost at random events and states of mind of the fifteen years preceding publication. The unity of the volume resides in the fact that each poem is a reflection of one or more facets of Apollinaire's psyche. Its evident variety suggests both the complexity of that focal centre and an act of volition which is in turn many-sided: in a letter written three months after the appearance of *Alcools* in April 1913, he declared: 'je prétends être un des pionniers de l'art varié' (*O.C.*, iv, 760). To have chosen only fifty poems from fifteen years' output and to have rearranged them in an order other than chronological was not simply, therefore, a way of covering his tracks or of satisfying his reticence, nor was it simply the result of a disorderly mind shuffling the pack and dealing according to the laws of chance: it was the product of his desire to achieve variety, to create order in disorder, to intrigue, surprise and win over his eventual reader. As such, it reflects an aesthetic preoccupation contemporaneous with the last stages of work on the book. Happily, poems written earlier could be fitted into such an accommodating scheme although they stemmed from a quite different—and relatively speaking immature— poetics. It could flex to changes of subject, tone and versification without its elasticity perishing, and so achieves Apollinaire's end. Implicit is an indication to reader or critic that to appreciate the volume aesthetically he need neither indulge his interest in bio-graphical chronology nor presuppose that, beyond the poet's complicated psychological unity and the variety principle, lies a conscious preoccupation with some Baudelairean 'architecture secrète'.

To a correspondent, Apollinaire wrote of *Alcools*: 'Vous le classerez dans l'école poétique qui vous plaira, je ne prétends faire partie d'aucune, mais il n'en est aucune également à laquelle je ne me sente un peu attaché' (*O.C.*, iv, 783). This curious mixture of a sense of independence and originality alongside a susceptibility to every outside influence that blows his voracious way is entirely characteristic. At the same time he realises in the first part of his sentence that the volume must stand to be judged on its own merits: once published it has its own independence separate from the poet. Reference back to him or outside itself in any way beyond the normal referential and connotational content of words is special pleading. Valéry's famous statement 'Mes vers ont le sens qu'on leur prête' is in this sense axiomatic. And while background information may be paraded as exhibits for our scrutiny and consequently affect our final judgement, it must be remembered that circumstantial evidence can never be the whole truth. Burns did not write 'O my love is like a red red rose' because it was short-lived and prickly. Yet Apollinaire has been particularly vulnerable to this sort of approach, and partly through his own fault.

The crucial recognition of the difference between literal and poetic truth relates directly to a further matter central to Apollinaire's poetry, namely the incorporation of contemporary events and discoveries in the necessary renewal of the lyrical tradition. While recognising that 'le lyrisme doit se renouveler avec chaque génération (*O.C.*, iv, 134), Apollinaire is aware of the danger of relying too exclusively on novelty: 'Chaque œuvre d'art doit trouver en elle-même sa logique, sa vraisemblance et non pas seulement dans les aspects fugitifs de la vie contemporaine' (*O.C.*, iv, 141). We therefore need to make with him (cf. *O.C.*, iv, 405) a distinction between the notions 'recent' and 'modern'. The first selects solely on a historical basis and covers what is novel or happens to be new by virtue of its being recently invented or produced. The second is a further selection made from among such recent things and designed to characterise a new mode of expression of certain enduring features of man's mind and actions. The first is gratuitous and/or fortuitous; the second is fundamental to the expression of man's existence in time. To be modern inevitably includes an awareness of the past as T. S. Eliot insists in 'Tradition and the Individual Talent', since being and becoming are inextricably linked: 'La meilleure façon d'être classique et pondéré est d'être de son temps en ne sacrifiant rien de ce que les Anciens ont pu nous apprendre' (*O.C.*, iv, 675). Tradition, when viewed in this light, is bound up with invention in art; works of durable quality will not be created if novelty is allowed to dominate *in vacuo*. Apollinaire's recognition of the importance of both tradition and invention was therefore entirely valid, but he had an unhappy tendency to over-emphasise one or the other at different times in his highly impressionable way. He was always looking for the right balance and adopted apparently contradictory stances both in theoretical statements and in poetic practice. Order and adventure are nonetheless the poles between which his poetry shuttles, and in craving the reader's indulgence, Apollinaire closes *Calligrammes* by declaring his interest:

Je sais d'ancien et de nouveau autant qu'un homme seul pourrait des deux savoir
...
Je juge cette longue querelle de la tradition et de l'invention
De l'Ordre et de l'Aventure

* * *

'Zone', one of the longest and most discussed poems in the collection, brings us face to face with an overtly autobiographical work and with an attempted ordering of adventure. Should it also be taken to suggest a framework of self-disclosure, whether direct or oblique, for the whole volume? As such it would certainly justify the variety of tone and topic, of form and facet that the poet explores and reveals. Whether viewed as welcome surprise or random inconsequentiality, this variety within a romantico-symbolist ambience is a keynote of the collection. What is more 'Zone' circumscribes the variety in several ways and adumbrates certain themes and attitudes despite its (self-)consciously 'modernist' approach.

Our first reaction can hardly help being surprise:

A la fin tu es las de ce monde ancien

Who is this poet who presumes to address us with such familiarity? What right does he have to suppose that we share his *ennui* or his iconoclasm? Apollinaire has arrested our attention and draws us towards a second phase of surprise, investigating the first more closely. Why, given the apparent rejection of established values, does he express himself in a traditional alexandrine, attributing to 'ancien' a conventional but uncolloquial three syllables? The paradox continues to unfurl. Why hasn't he put a full-stop at the end of the line? The eye moves to the second line:

Bergère ô tour Eiffel le troupeau des ponts bêle ce matin

What sort of a rhyming couplet does this make? Why does he mix a traditional pastoral image with that girdered loin of recent

times, the Eiffel Tower? How can he want both the overthrow of
'ce monde ancien' and the rhetorical advantage of an internal
pair of hexasyllables rhyming perfectly for the ear ('Eiffel' ...
'bêle')?

It soon becomes apparent that Apollinaire is addressing himself
as 'tu' and that the paradox is an expression of the conflict
within his own mind. On the one hand lies an inventive
urge made up of a positive side—adventurousness, individual-
istic self-expression, the acceptance of recently-introduced
phenomena—and a negative one—iconoclasm, faddishness, a
weathercock's capacity to turn to every modish '-ism'. On the
other hand lies a deep fascination with and knowledge of traditional cultural products and values, a profound longing for
order. The tension between order and adventure was but rarely
resolved: indeed often in his search for order he fell into unad-
venturous pastiche and in his search for adventure into disorderly posturing. But at his delicately-poised best he can be
enchanting, tapping a lyrical vein with fresh vitality and finding
the words and rhythms that have made him one of the most
popular of modern French poets.

Despite its importance, 'Zone' does not really achieve that
balance, though it remains exciting. Presented in terms of a walk
from the centre of Paris to Apollinaire's home in the suburb of
Auteuil, the poem traces a day in the poet's life, from one
morning to dawn the next day, during which he notes certain
immediate events and impressions, reminisces about his life so far
and meditates particularly on his attitude towards religion in the
context of passing time. The texture of the writing is discursive—
one might say peripatetic—using a Symbolist mixture of rhyme
and assonance, pararhyme and dissonance. There are many
syncretistic juxtapositions and opaque references, and
Apollinaire runs the risk of any modernist poetry, that, as
Michael Hamburger puts it in *The Truth of Poetry* (p. 80), of
coming to terms with its contemporaneous universe but not
surviving 'its occasions and phenomena'. Is his view of religion,
for example, bold, naive or tasteless? 'La religion seule est restée
toute neuve la religion / Est restée simple comme les hangars de
Port-Aviation' (ll. 5–6) and 'le Christ ... monte au ciel mieux
que les aviateurs / Il détient le record du monde pour la hauteur'

(ll. 40–1). Apollinaire recaptures here a child's sense of wonder, amuses us with a kind of banner headline, but also leaves us somewhat ill at ease. A Roman Catholic training permits such boldness in a way perhaps distasteful to the Protestant palate. But can Pius X really be called modern just because he blessed a French pioneer of aviation? Surely the poet's irony bites deeper, losing itself perhaps in obscurity. For this reactionary pope, as Apollinaire could not have failed to know, condemned as heretical a movement known as 'le modernisme'. Beyond the recent phenomena there is nonetheless real modernity in Apollinaire's evocation of the city. His total acceptance of his urban setting as legitimate subject-matter for poetry means that he can follow Baudelaire's tracks and see poetry in posters and grace (in both senses) in an industrial street. (Interestingly enough, Mallarmé specifically excluded posters from his concept of poetry, as is recorded by Jules Huret in his *Enquête sur l'évolution littéraire*.) The timeless down-and-outs join the equally timeless prostitutes in the poet's word-picture of Paris: such subjects are not taboo for him and help him to look beyond the surface of contingencies.

He presents the apotheosis of his century by repeated reference to the aeroplane. Rather as in 'Vendémiaire' rivers of wine pour their tribute to Paris, so here birds flock from all points of history and the globe to fraternise with 'la volante machine' (l. 70). It is an acceptable culmination to the episode which had started with Apollinaire recalling the intense piety of his childhood: 'Vous priez toute la nuit dans la chapelle du collège' (l. 30). Yet we come back to earth with a bump, and the poem never again reaches such a pitch of self-induced exhilaration. The aeroplane disappears from the sky and from the poem, and we are left trailing the poet across Paris. The skeleton of the neo-classical unities of time, place and action combined, clothed in the three-fold narrative, is hard put to it, with shocks such as this, to avoid severe distortion or even disintegration. Striving perhaps to do too much and in a manner new to him, Apollinaire loses sight for too long at a time of the different threads of his narrative and imagery. His autobiographical account unfurls in the timeless present of memory ('Maintenant …', ll. 71, 89; 'Te voici …', ll. 106–9, etc.) but the point of return to the narrator's true present is unclear: is it after a past tense has made its appearance (i.e. after line 118) or just before a future tense occurs (in line 144)? And do the random peripatetic elements of the second half of the poem match the excitement generated by the interweaving of references and images in the first?

Any pioneer runs a risk. It would seem that Apollinaire banked here on a lyrical gesture both confessional and dramatic which after the initial *élan* lapsed more and more into the documentation of his identity. By confusing his own 'I' with the 'I' of the poem, he forfeits his lyrical and aesthetic advantage. For just as sincerity cannot be a criterion for the critic, so it cannot be a sufficient cohesive and structuring force for the poet.

'Zone' cannot, however, be lightly dismissed. Apollinaire obviously attached importance to it by placing it at the opening of the volume, and many critics have paid it close attention and praised it highly. It focuses attention on Apollinaire as poet of the sometimes aimless but always urgent search and sets this in a spatio-temporal continuum which offers such magical properties as omniscience and illuminism to the poet convinced of his special powers of insight. Certainly it contains some impressive as well as some revealing writing even if Apollinaire was to admit 'je ne me rappelle plus un vers de "Zone"' (*O.C.*, iv, 493). It succeeds, for example, in so far as there is 'opposition à la description' (*O.C.*, iv, 281). This phrase occurs, applied to his own poetry among others, in a piece Apollinaire wrote shortly after the first appearance of 'Zone' in *Les Soirées de Paris* in December 1912 and his correction of the proofs of *Alcools* the same month. That it applies directly to 'Zone' seems probable from certain verbal connections one can make between the poem and the prose piece, for example:

> Tu lis les prospectus les catalogues les affiches qui chantent tout haut
> Voilà la poésie ce matin et pour la prose il y a les journaux
>
> (ll. 11–12)

> Picasso et Braque introduisaient dans leurs œuvres d'art des lettres d'enseignes et d'autres inscriptions, parce que, dans une ville moderne, l'inscription, l'enseigne, la publicité jouent un rôle artistique très important et parce qu'elles s'adaptent à cette fin. (*O.C.*, iv, 282)

A clear and brief example of the poet's opposition to description can show how a line can be tightened up to a pitch of great intensity. In the magazine version, the last line reads: 'Soleil levant cou tranché'. But in the definitive text, after the autobiography, after the nostalgia of a Christian consciousness, after the sympathetic view of Paris nearing the end of the *belle époque*, comes a last line of shattering power: 'Soleil cou coupé'. Not only is it a striking visual image of the rising sun, it also contains concise elements of violence both in sound and sense that suggest the end of an era rather than the beginning of day. But it is less a prophecy of the Great War than the sad ending to what Apollinaire admits to be 'ce poème de fin d'amour' (*O.C.*, iv, 491). His six-year liaison with Marie Laurencin had come to an end; such violence as he felt was verbalised and concentrated into the last three words of the poem.

Elsewhere it is simply his sadness that shows, and in the second poem, 'Le Pont Mirabeau', the same lost love is celebrated, but in a different key and with a poignant simplicity enhanced by the choice of a folk-ballad presentation. The haunting refrain tolls the passage of time and continues the tone of simple universality established by the verses of statement and understatement. To say that it has the qualities of so many anonymous traditional ballads and that it in its turn has inspired many composers to set it to music suggests that Apollinaire has managed to epitomise a familiar moment in every man's life. By linking it to a bridge over the Seine, he also enlists the sentiments (and sentimentality) of those for whom Paris has some intangible charm. Exploiting the well-worn image of a river to symbolise time flowing relentlessly by, he echoes many an expression of regret which may feed his reader's nostalgia. If he strikes an uncharacteristic pose of perhaps slightly fey offended innocence, all is forgiven for his expression of a real and profoundly communicable sadness: it is perfect anthology material. One need not dwell on the mellifluous fluidity of the lines nor on the high proportion of feminine rhymes and of sounds that let one softly linger that create this effect. For this poem perhaps more than any other in Apollinaire calls not for dissection but for re-reading and memorisation. It achieves that magical inversion of all successful poetry of suffering, kindling aesthetic joy from the tinder of exposed emotions: one is reminded of Baudelaire's declaration in his essay on Théophile Gautier: 'C'est un des privilèges prodigieux de l'Art que l'horrible, artistement exprimé, devienne beauté et que la *douleur* rhythmée et cadencée remplisse l'esprit d'une *joie* calme.' At the beginning of March 1912, Apollinaire wrote more self-centredly: 'je suis la tristesse même, mais non la vilaine et pauvre tristesse qui assombrit tout. La mienne brille comme une étoile, elle illumine le chemin de l'Art à travers l'effroyable nuit de la vie' (*O.C.*, iv, 916). Over three years later, in a letter to Madeleine Pagès, he was to insist: 'il ne faut point voir de tristesse dans mon œuvre, mais la vie même, avec une constante et consciente volupté de vivre, de connaître, de voir, de savoir et d'exprimer' (*O.C.*, iv, 505). The pleasures of the senses, of the mind and of words are well-established features of poetic sensibility. When, in addition, there is the formal orderliness of 'Le Pont Mirabeau', one well understands how Apollinaire can agree with the traditional view expressed by a critic friend: 'Vous avez eu raison d'insister sur la nécessité … d'une contrainte intérieure, qui est indispensable à toute poésie, c'est-à-dire à toute création; il est juste aussi de ramener "l'étrange magie des mots" à son rôle de moyen poétique' (*O.C.*, iv, 886).

Yet where in all this is Apollinaire the iconoclast, Apollinaire the pace-setter, Apollinaire the adventurer? Half of him seems to be missing. The one feature that betokens his modernity is the lack of punctuation. Yet after the initial surprise and the occasional fumbling this causes, and the recognition of its potential in the creation of syntactical ambiguity (as in line 2) and of fluidity, we can surely agree with Apollinaire's own view: 'Pour ce qui concerne la ponctuation je ne l'ai supprimée que parce qu'elle m'a paru inutile et elle l'est en effet, le rythme même et la coupe des vers voilà la véritable ponctuation et il n'en est point besoin d'une autre' (*O.C.*, iv, 768). Apart from the fact that his punctuation was idiosyncratic to the point of being slapdash in his prose, the gratuitous nature of this element of surprise prompts us to wonder why he thought it worthwhile to suppress almost all his dots and commas in the very last stages of the production of his book. It is difficult not to see it as the reaction of an easily-influenced character to Marinetti's recommendation to do so in his Futurist manifesto, the relevant parts of which were presented in French in the *Mercure de France* only two months before Apollinaire corrected the proofs of *Alcools* for the same publishing house.

Far more central to an investigation of Apollinaire's poetry is the evidence that the first two poems, however different, both celebrate in a minor key the end of a love-affair. Apollinaire is indeed much less a love poet than a poet of lost love, and 'La Chanson du mal-aimé' continues this theme while referring in fact to a different girl, to Annie Playden instead of Marie Laurencin. His sense of variety brings, after the formal and brief minuet of 'Le Pont Mirabeau', a long romance with contrasting interludes. With the saddened lucidity of hindsight, he appends an epigraph which shows his recognition of his capacity to fall in and out of love and introduces the traditional image of the phoenix reborn from its own ashes which is to figure notably in 'Le Brasier' with multiple connotations.

Structurally, the poem consists of a main narrative divided into four sections by three interpolated episodes which are an integral part of the ensemble. They act as brief but striking flashbacks in an almost cinematic sequence. A five-line stanza (the 'quintil') is used throughout with a consistent pattern of rhymes or assonance, and this visibly anchors the poem to a tradition so that Apollinaire is free to reserve his audacity for other things. As in 'Zone' the narrative framework is a walk across part of a city or rather, in this case, two cities, London and Paris, between which the poem is slung like a necklace with three large bloodstones interspersed with smaller ones. As in 'Zone' too, this framework is simply a basis for further exploration of the disparate mind and memory of the poet: it allows total liberty of reference while retaining a sense of order. Thus, like 'Zone' again, it is an interesting guide to Apollinaire's psyche but runs the risk of collapsing as poetry. In fact, 'La Chanson du mal-aimé' is more successful: it has an imaginative and not simply a peripatetic narrative coherence and indeed shows both more daring and more balance. It is marred only, perhaps, by Apollinaire's apparent inability to prevent himself parading his scraps of knowledge: if, like Autolycus, he is 'a snapper-up of unconsidered trifles', he is also an inveterate Jack Horner.

On a misty London night, the narrator, obsessed by the desire to meet his belovèd, seems to see her loom up in various forms which he promptly pursues:

> Un voyou qui ressemblait à
> Mon amour vint à ma rencontre
> ...
> Une femme lui ressemblant
> ...
> Sortit saoule d'une taverne

He sees himself as Pharaoh chasing the Israelites in vain, as he clutches at shadows and is at last persuaded of the vanity of his search for true love. He is no Odysseus with a patient Penelope, no Dushyanta with a faithful Ṣakuntala but, like Aragon's 'Richard II quarante', might say: 'Je reste roi de mes douleurs'. Indeed, like Shakespeare's Richard II, having lost everything he is in search of an identity. The somewhat extravagant range of reference is unified around the concept of kingship, but this is no consolation: he is obliged to face his separation squarely. Having done so, he is able to evoke the fresh joy of his former love in the first interlude, 'Aubade chantée à Laetare un an passé'. In tones of pastoral innocence the aubade utterly changes the mood: the 'rosy-fingered dawn' of spring encourages naked pink gods-cum-rose-petals to sport to the accompaniment of Pan's pipes and the fantasia of euphoric frogs. The clichés are intended, a by-product of subsequent disenchantment. Even if the episode were originally written separately in all seriousness, its incorporation in a broader context gives it this more acceptable ironic perspective. Now 'Beaucoup de ces dieux ont péri' (l. 86) and the narrator returns to his regret in a passage echoing the opening section in some details (compare l. 98 with l. 20) and resuming its sense (as in 'Je reste fidèle et dolent', l. 100) but essentially linking the 'Aubade' to the next interlude, 'Réponse des cosaques zaporogues au sultan de Constantinople'. This stands as an extreme example, forcefully expressed, of fidelity to a cause: the Sultan demands the cossacks' allegiance to Islam and to himself. They reply with a string of insults well chosen to offend a Moslem's sensibilities, peppering their abuse with references which are still some of the most offensive to Mohammedan ears, maligning the Sultan's mother and relating him to a pig.

No attempt is made to link this episode with what follows.

Instead Apollinaire repeats a verse from the end of the opening section, a verse which will be repeated again to start the final section. Another stanza from the second narrative section also closes the poem. Such staging-posts help to structure the poem but also accrue significance with each repetition, coming to express the two poles of the poet's attention, one the star of the lost love he follows, the other his own poetic production, 'La romance du mal-aimé' (ll. 94 and 294). After expressing his unhappiness in a variety of black and white images and others linked with flow, fire and death (all deriving ultimately, if indirectly, from the opening cluster of the Milky Way)— 'candide', 'colombe', 'blanche rade', 'marguerite'; 'pyraustes', 'feux follets', 'bûcher' etc.—a striking if arbitrary comparison sparks off recollections, real or imagined, of buggery:

> Et moi j'ai le cœur aussi gros
> Qu'un cul de dame damascène
> (ll. 196–7)

From Apollinaire's correspondence, notably with Lou, it is apparent that he had a particular taste for anal intercourse (still a crime in English law): his attentions to Annie Playden and Marie Laurencin in this respect have already been noted (see pp. 3, 7 above). The reference here to the relevant part of the lady's anatomy consequently arouses the narrator's dormant passion and sets fire to the arcane erotic arsenal of the third interlude, 'Les Sept Epées'. The passage is further tied in with a sense of grief by the connection of 'Sept épées de mélancolie … ô claires douleurs … dans mon cœur' (ll. 201–3) with the traditional Christian symbolism of seven swords piercing the heart of Our Lady of Sorrows: Apollinaire's syncretistic analogising trampled roughshod over the niceties of congruity and implied good taste and he was to bequeath this capacity to the surrealists and their inheritors. No genteel understatement is allowed to temper the poet's avowal of his suffering, and in this perhaps he catches the disproportion of a frustrated lover's recriminations. Yet humour is apparent even in the play on 'gros', switching from metaphorical to literal meaning, in line 196 quoted above. 'Les Sept Epées' is a Rabelaisian verbal flourish sufficiently unambiguous to make the general purport clear despite the obscurities and private neologisms: each sword is given particular phallic overtones apparently to correspond to different states and capacities of the male organ. Further details would not be appropriate to the present work.[1] The final section opens and closes on stanzas already presented and picks up threads of earlier imagery while shifting the setting of the end to Paris from the London of the beginning. Royalty appears again, this time as one of the 'nageurs morts', and the connection between the stars and destiny is given special attention. If Paris is gay and sparkling where London was its proverbially foggy self, there is no consolation. The narrator wanders across it 'Sans avoir le cœur de mourir' (l. 275) but nonetheless haunted by the song of a passion which is past but refuses to die.

Writing of the poem some twelve years after it was composed, Apollinaire admitted that he had been unjust to Annie and recognised his part in the failure of their relationship:

> ... bien des expressions de ce poème sont trop sévères et injurieuses pour une fille qui ne comprenait rien à moi et qui m'aima puis fut déconcertée d'aimer un poète être fantasque; je l'aimai charnellement mais nos esprits étaient loin l'un de l'autre. ... le mariage était impossible, et tout s'arrangea par son départ en Amérique, mais j'en souffris beaucoup, témoin ce poème où je me croyais mal aimé tandis que c'était moi qui aimais mal ... (*O.C.*, iv, 492–3)

Some of the poem's dramatic power derives from its excessive attitudes: passion is rarely concerned with the balanced scales of justice. Yet because of its concentration on the poet's reactions and not on the 'fault' of the object of his passion, such disproportion assumes its own psychological rationale. What is more the controlled but supple flow of the stanzaic presentation suggests emotion recollected in tranquility rather than logorrhoea, and the extreme postures are reserved for the interludes which thereby show the intensity of the feelings the poet had known, counterpoint them with the relative stoicism or resignation of the body of the poem, and give a measure of justification to such distraught and irrational sentiments as are there expressed. Apollinaire dares a great deal in 'La Chanson du mal-aimé', and the fact that this ambition was matched both by an overriding passion and by an adequate poetic form makes it one of his finest achievements and takes him out of the 'minor poet' category to

which shorter if more perfect lyric pieces such as 'Le Pont
Mirabeau' would otherwise have consigned him. In theme and
treatment it achieves a blend of the modern and the traditional
which makes it both palatable and exciting, and last but by no
means least reveals an authentic and individual voice.

* * *

For reasons of space it is obviously not possible to pay close
attention to all the fifty poems of *Alcools*. Having presented some
considerations of a general order at the start of this chapter and
analysed the first three poems in the collection, I propose to
devote time now to a selection from the remaining poems which
illustrate other aspects of Apollinaire's art or are of particular
literary interest. Many of the short poems do not seem to require
special elucidation. Omission does not necessarily mean condemnation, though I believe that some pieces (e.g. 'Palais') are
frankly third-rate.

'Chantre', for a one-line poem, has received a remarkable
amount of critical attention. André Rouveyre devoted fourteen
pages to it in *Amour et poésie d'Apollinaire*, but its main value seems
to be its disorientating surprise. After a relatively serious
sequence including the longest poem in the book, its monocord
humour and looking-glass logic offer light relief. Once the play
on 'cordeau' as 'cor d'eau' has been noted it seems inappropriate
to be ponderous. 'La Maison des morts', although much longer,
need not detain us either except to note that its prosaic narrative
betrays its genesis as a short story simply chopped up into flat
free verse. Doubtless in its original prose presentation it had its
flights of poetic fancy: as poetry it is pedestrian but provides
another voice for our versatile ventriloquist.

'Cortège' is altogether more interesting. It is a self-exploration
presented in terms of people, things and ideas passing before
Apollinaire's mind's eye (and other senses). The early lines are
marked by the repetition of reference to a mythical bird, the
closing ones by two rhyming quatrains, and these structuring
devices help hold the poem together. The poet, *homo duplex*,
recognises his Baudelairean capacity to step outside himself in a
way which anticipates Supervielle's treatment of the theme:[2]

> Un jour je m'attendais moi-même
> Je me disais Guillaume il est temps que tu viennes
> Pour que je sache enfin celui-là que je suis
>
> (ll. 20–2)

His sense of empathy is similarly no less than Baudelaire's, at least *in potentia*:

> Moi qui connais les autres
> Je les connais par les cinq sens et quelques autres
>
> (ll. 23–4)

The so-called sixth sense, intuition, would certainly be high on the poet's list of 'quelques autres', being Apollinaire's sense par excellence ('peut-être ma seule qualité', as he wrote to Lou: see p. 7 above). Yet while the five senses are illustrated with examples, definite priority being given to sight (ll. 25–32) and smell (ll. 33–9), the reader is left to intuit in his turn the poet's 'other' senses through an imaginative exploration of various enigmatic juxtapositions and analogies. Apollinaire is he who can write

> Et je m'éloignerai m'illuminant au milieu d'ombres
>
> (l. 10)

with a fierce sense of poetic pride and yet reveal soon after a touching modesty in avoiding self-infatuation:

> Je me disais Guillaume il est temps que tu viennes
> Et d'un lyrique pas s'avançaient ceux que j'aime
> Parmi lesquels je n'étais pas
>
> (ll. 49–51)

He adds up to 'the sum of his lacks':[3]

> Le cortège passait et j'y cherchais mon corps
> Tous ceux qui survenaient et n'étaient pas moi-même
> Amenaient un à un les morceaux de moi-même
> On me bâtit peu à peu comme on élève un tour
> Les peuples s'entassaient et je parus moi-même
> Qu'ont formé tous les corps et les choses humaines
>
> (ll. 60–5)

In the obsessional and inelegant repetition of 'moi-même' at the line-endings, Apollinaire shows himself acutely aware of the psychological and consequent artistic dangers inherent in the apparently desirable power of empathy. His capacity to project himself into others or to identify with them creates an identity crisis for himself. Is he merely a collection of fragments shored against his own ruins? Is he a hole to be filled in by those around him (like the Hermit in James Saunders' *Next Time I'll Sing to You*)? Proteus had his problems. Apollinaire's solution here is to turn away from the blank void of the future to a past which offers the comforting thought of certain tangible achievements. He closes on some classically balanced and sententious alexandrines:

> Près du passé luisant demain est incolore
> Il est informe aussi près de ce qui parfait
> Présente tout ensemble et l'effort et l'effet
> (ll. 71–3)

Apollinaire's quest for self-knowledge in 'Cortège' and his very awareness of an identity problem enlist our sympathy. That he can stand back from himself and as it were watch contributions being made to his personality is psychologically of the highest interest, and both friends and critics have seen a positively *mimetic* capacity (even to sounding like the last person he had been with, preaching the gospel according to the latest book he had read) at work in his character and writings. Its implications will be further considered in the last chapter of this book. For the moment it is sufficient to see how a personal matter—as opposed to a private one[4]—is an entirely proper subject for poetry, and how this poem is an expression in its theme of the psycho-perceptual stage of the creative process and in its realisation of the communication of that insight. Stretched to breaking-point between an amorphous heap and the light and flight of poetic vision, Apollinaire holds himself tense and conveys that tension to us. Even if not every detail seems relevant to his purpose, the overall form serves the general intention, a peripatetic element (here the 'cortège' of both sense-impressions and people) allowing, as in 'Zone' and 'La Chanson du mal-aimé', some randomness of reference.

'Marizibill', more compact and less ambitious, is one of several successful short lyrics in *Alcools*. It displays an agreeable lightness of touch and while drawing a moral is not moralising in tone. Nor does it show any coy or prudish inhibitions in its evocation of a Cologne prostitute who comes to symbolise those who lack conviction and fibre. It embodies without undue insistence an attitude to life in an uncomplicated lyricism imbued with tradition, and these appealing if somewhat lightweight qualities characterise many of Apollinaire's brief poems. Together they undoubtedly form the core of his poetic work and they may be read, as they were generally written, with facility. Thus the poems grouped as 'Rhénanes', inspired by Apollinaire's stay in the Rhineland in 1901–2, and the sequence 'A la Santé', provoked by his incarceration in La Santé prison in 1911 and heavy with echoes of Verlaine's prison-poems in *Sagesse*, seem if anything not to call for internal dissection so much as for extraneous explication. The short lyrics usually share some features of a family likeness, whether of form (the 'quintil' used in 'La Chanson du mal-aimé' reappears in 'Marizibill', 'Marie', 'Lul de Faltenin', 'Rosemonde' and 'Cors de chasse' as well as in the opening section of 'Le Brasier' and with variant rhyme- or assonance-schemes in 'Adieu' and 'Les Sapins'), of subject (fleeting time, lost love, resigned sadness often linked with a predilection for autumnal imagery) or of tone (stemming from the poet's habitual recourse to a definable range of form and subject). Things past, things missing: these haunt Apollinaire's sensibilities and allow his qualification as an elegiac poet. That he was more than simply that (through, for example, his sense of humour and of immediacy) underlines the unwisdom of over-neat categorisation. That he saw himself also as a magus is apparent from some of the longer poems which we must now investigate.

Neither 'Le Voyageur', with its stream-of-half-consciousness technique anticipating 'Zone' and surrealism, nor 'Poème lu au mariage d'André Salmon'—despite its claim that 'fondés en poésie nous avons des droits sur les paroles qui forment et défont l'Univers' (l. 36) and its reference to Orpheus (l. 17)—embodies the magus approach: they remain too closely linked to mundane circumstance. 'Merlin et la vieille femme', on the same theme and with the same literary and legendary origins as Apollinaire's story 'L'Enchanteur pourrissant', would seem to suggest an interest in a magus-figure, but the poet is content to recount his narrative in verse as if from the outside. Powers of insight and divination attributed to the sage and sorcerer of Arthurian legend are not directly claimed for the poet. Yet the attraction of the magus is evident, just as it is in 'Le Larron', a more complex and obscure work where the thief is a multiplex character suggesting Christ, Orpheus, a prophet, a poet and Apollinaire himself. Precise interpretation seems impossible with such arcane syncretism, and it may well be that the obscurantism is a heritage from the Symbolist aesthetic. There would nevertheless seem to be a voice struggling to declare its approval of the poet as magus, and this voice is heard more clearly in 'L'Ermite'. Another versified narrative, it contains some amusing word-play (sometimes overdone) and references to contained sexuality familiar from maturer and richer works. Both the sense of separateness from other men and the expression of frustration through sexual reference are relevant to the total picture of Apollinaire's view of the *poète-voyant*. And its humour participates in making it palatable through a measure of ironic detachment evident in such phrases as 'Je suis unicorne' (l. 21) and 'Ma migraine pieuse' (l. 80) and indeed in the very narrative substance where piety and propriety just manage to confine the urges of lust.

The multivalency of the magus-figure is further presented in the fourth of this interrupted sequence of long poems. The characteristics of Apollinaire's Merlin, Thief and Hermit—outsiders from society, bearing a special burden but also a special message, threatened with extinction but implicitly assured of ressuscitation in one form or another—are shared by 'L'Emigrant de Landor Road'. While the allusion in the title to Annie Playden's London address clarifies the autobiographical element in the poem, it cannot be said to contain its meaning as Décaudin suggests (*Dossier*, p. 170). Rather is 'L'Emigrant' the significant word. For in its fundamental features it is linked precisely with the characteristics of the magus listed above. In the event a particular farewell—a kind of death—prompts the profound sense of loss and transfers the real, fundamental departure from Annie to Apollinaire himself: the title, after all, is not 'L'Emigrante de Landor Road'. It is the poet who is doomed to wander and suffer, but he too who has the chance of survival. In this respect it is instructive to consider the closing lines of these four poems presenting a magus-like character. 'Merlin et la vieille femme' ends: 'Je m'éterniserai sous l'aubépine en fleurs'. 'Le Larron' is told by the chorus: 'Tu n'as de signe que le signe de la croix'. A similar implication of life after death or life in death is present in 'la sainte cruauté des passiflores' which closes 'L'Ermite', passion-flowers being traditionally and symbolically associated with Christ's death. The hermit wants to change his worldly passions for an unworldly Passion. And at the end of 'L'Emigrant de Landor Road', after referring to a symbolic wedding of a man (the Doge of Venice) with the sea we have a twofold symbolic death:

> Des cadavres de jours rongés par les étoiles
> Parmi le bruit des flots et les derniers serments

(ll. 52–3)

Rebirth is nonetheless implicit: the cycle of day and night has come round to dawn (l. 51), and if the suffering is bound to continue, so is the struggle and so is the hope.

This magus-sequence continues and culminates in 'Le Brasier'. Apollinaire considered it one of his best poems (see *O.C.*, iv, 495) and of it wrote a sentence which has often been applied to the whole of his poetic output: 'Je ne cherche qu'un lyrisme neuf et humaniste à la fois' (*O.C.*, iv, 697). 'Le Brasier' puts the Orphic poet himself on stage as protagonist, dismissing the useful but partial *personae* of Merlin, thief, hermit and emigrant, and concentrates attention on his rebirth, so embodying 'le mythe de l'éternel retour'.[5] For the image that presides unspecified over the poem is that of the phoenix, the mythical bird which was said to arise from the funeral ashes of its previous incarnation. Implicit too is the claim that the poet is not simply, as certain nineteenth-century poets would have it, a high-priest of a sacred mystery, but victim and victor in that rite as well. The 'têtes de femmes' (l. 20) are not solely those of Apollinaire's past loves but also archetypal and largely inaccessible consorts: Eurydice, Aphrodite, Viviane and the hermit's and emigrant's elusive dreams. A sexual urge is intimately involved with the poet's creative instinct: '[le] hennissement mâle / Des centaures dans leurs haras' (ll. 8–9) cries firstly with the recognition that 'l'amour est devenu mauvais' (l. 13) and then at the cheering ranks of female heads. Divestment is therefore appropriate, but is more than physical: 'Mon âme au soleil se dévêt' (l. 15). No less appropriate is the proliferation of fire, death-dealing but rejuvenating, consuming life and death alike. Both 'De vives mains' (l. 3) and 'feu / Ce Passé' (ll. 3–4)—where Apollinaire plays ambiguously on the other meaning of *feu* 'late' (as in *feu le roi* 'the late king')—are thrown into the furnace which the poet carries about within him. Flames leap up across the countryside, not only as in a bush-fire, nor simply as symbols of the poet's spreading message, but also as in some surrealist image (such as Dali's 'Burning Giraffe') with echoes of Hieronymus Bosch. The power of art is greater than the inertia of matter; recalling the legend of Amphion so much akin to that of Orpheus, Apollinaire submits to 'tous les tons charmants / Qui rendent les pierres agiles' (ll. 24–5). In the first part of the poem, then, the poet metaphorically throws himself (both past and present) on the judgement of the flames in the conviction that he can thereby better discharge his destiny.

The second section relates the ordeal by fire taking place and immediately shows the poet passing muster: 'Je flambe dans le brasier à l'ardeur adorable' (l. 26). Evidently proud of his consequent distinction from ordinary mortals—'Il n'y a plus rien de commun entre moi / Et ceux qui craignent les brûlures' (ll. 41–2)—he revels in adding fuel: 'Je suffis pour l'éternité à entretenir le feu de mes délices' (l. 30). After his call in the opening section: 'Qu'au brasier les flammes renaissent' (l. 14), he is himself now reborn: 'Voici ma vie renouvelée' (l. 36), and when these last three words are repeated three lines later, they are followed by conclusive evidence that the 'brasier' is his very life within himself: 'Ses flammes sont immenses' (l. 40). The critical passage, a *rite de passage*, shows Apollinaire paying particular attention to the sound-play of words: 'L'ardeur adorable' (l. 26), 'm' and nasals in line 27, 'membres'—'flambent' (l. 28), 'l'éternité à entretenir' (l. 30) etc. Such attention, creative of tension, is relaxed in the third section where from an armchair firmly implanted on this earth the poet reviews the extraordinary spectacle. A number of references recall the previous sections: 'le ver Zamir' ('qui sans outils pouvait bâtir le temple de Jérusalem, quelle saisissante image du poète!', *O.C.*, iii, 822) harks back to

Amphion; the sun reappears after being eclipsed by the flames and protected from their superior power by the wings of birds (presumably phoenixes, alone able to withstand the heat); flames continue to lick around the poet like a living laurel-wreath of fire. He has seen the unity of the poet's position, straddling the necessary ambivalence of vision and reality. The riddles can be packed away: 'le troupeau de sphinx regagne la sphingerie' (l. 54), yet they will inevitably remain a constant attraction, since there will always be a need for the Orphic poet to sacrifice himself in the interests of rebirth and wholeness. Just as rivers on a globe seem to stitch the world together, Apollinaire declares himself ready to brave the burning fiery furnace of his vision to resolve at whatever cost the ambiguities of which he is here poignantly aware:

> J'aimerais mieux nuit et jour dans les sphingeries
> Vouloir savoir pour qu'enfin on m'y dévorât

> (ll. 66–7)

'Le Brasier' is Apollinaire's most extreme statement of the essence of the magus position. In its image structure it is also among the most coherent of his longer poems. If there is some simplistic romanticisation of the poet's role, it is due in part to the legacy of Romanticism and Symbolism. But that a poet should quite legitimately feel he had to justify his ways to man in the face of materialism, hostility and indifference is understandable. At the heart of his separateness, errancy and pride, he senses a burning desire which both consumes and consummates his being. If he can allow himself to be an elegiac or modernist poet according to mood, if he can, more precariously, indulge in mimicking the latest voice to come his way, he must assert, both for his own mental health and his reader's sympathy, his fundamental belief in his poetic vocation. The searing vision of 'Le Brasier' certainly requires the positive proof of less absolute and, as it were, less theoretical poems, but it underpins them forcibly as an Orphic manifesto.

'Les Fiançailles'—'nul doute qu'avec "Le Brasier" il ne soit mon meilleur poème sinon le plus immédiatement accessible' (*O.C.*, iv, 495)—pursues the theme of the alchemical furnace but in a more dissipated medley of tone and reference. The quest seems to have tipped into slightly inebriated self-satisfaction and 'ce bûcher le nid de mon courage' on which the poem ends seems to imply borrowed—even Dutch—rather than genuine courage. 'Je buvais à plein verre les étoiles' (l. 13) perhaps explains but scarcely justifies the poet's inability to avoid tottering between pomposity and vulgarity. Bathos is apparent in some of the analogies (e.g. 'C'est la lune qui cuit comme un œuf sur le plat', l. 79), but proportion is lost by overstated claims ('Et porteur de soleils je brûle au centre de deux nébuleuses', l. 32) and hollow self-aggrandisement ('J'ai eu le courage de regarder en arrière', l. 37; 'si le temps venait où l'ombre enfin solide / Se multipliait en réalisant la diversité formelle de mon amour / J'admirerais mon ouvrage', ll. 55-7). The valid question 'Comment comment réduire / L'infiniment petite science / Que m'imposent mes sens' (ll. 60-2) seems not to find a satisfactory answer here. And if this is the best his new aesthetic can produce we are unlikely to be sympathetic to the false modesty of his plea:

> Pardonnez-moi mon ignorance
> Pardonnez-moi de ne plus connaître l'ancien jeu des vers
> (ll. 49-50)

If we continue to tread solely on the stepping-stones of the longer poems, however, 'Les Fiançailles', dedicated to Picasso and perhaps attempting to reproduce in words some of his techniques of fragmentation, leads thematically from 'Le Brasier' to 'Vendémiaire'. From Orphic, he becomes poetically Bacchic. 'Vendémiaire', named after the month in the French Revolutionary calendar when the *vendanges* took place, also links up with the zodiac sign Virgo referred to in 'Les Fiançailles' as a further exploration of Apollinaire's 'saison mentale' ('Signe'). It furthermore underlines the poet's French patriotism and particular affection for Paris by having the various regions and provincial towns pay a cumulative liquid tribute to the capital. Like the poet, Paris has an insatiable thirst and swallows the 'boissons vivantes' and 'gouttes tièdes' which are offered. Apollinaire assimilates himself totally to Paris, becoming its voice, its throat: 'Ecoutez-moi je suis le gosier de Paris' (l. 169); 'Je suis ivre d'avoir bu tout l'univers' (l. 167). The constant crescendo and insistent accelerando as Brittany, Flanders, Provence, Rhone and Rhine pour the juice of their grapes down the capital's/ poet's ever-open gullet is as closely organised and appealing as Dukas's 'L'Apprenti sorcier' or Ravel's 'Boléro'. It makes an appropriate flourish as an ending to a volume entitled *Alcools*.

In many ways, however, it is not typical of the collection. It is more single- (or simple-) minded, more obviously coherent than most of the other long poems, more convivial and rumbustious than the rest. Was Apollinaire determined to end on a positive, hopeful note, by contrast with the self-pity and melancholy that inform most of the volume? Is the optimism of 'Vendémiaire' meant to counterbalance the pessimism of 'Zone'? It is possible, but Apollinaire was not the careful planner of an architecture that Baudelaire was: there is no traceable progression from one pole to another. Indeed 'Cors de chasse' underlines a balance but not an opposition, being a clear echo of 'Le Pont Mirabeau'. Rather is there a purposeful mixing of poems, long and short, dejected and forward-looking, quasi-medieval and futurist, with the aim of entertaining the reader and projecting a complex *persona* living the tensions, frustrations and excitements of *belle époque* Paris. That such a mask should borrow certain features of its wearer's face is scarcely surprising but, as we have seen, it can on occasion be self-sufficient. If it bears traces of its encounters with other minds and other masks, lines from other poet's faces, scars from accidents and surgery, it nonetheless retains the quiddity of a recognisable personality. *Alcools* is Apollinaire's scrapbook pasted up anew to give variety. Like most scrapbooks it is the record of a person and a period and holds most interest for the compiler's friends when anecdotal material accompanies its presentation. But this one contains some treasures which need no anecdotes to survive both the poet and his friends.

III

'CALLIGRAMMES'

While *Alcools* is a medley on the dominant theme of the self with particular reference to love's labours lost and creativity, *Calligrammes* is unified in several ways. Firstly, its presentation is essentially chronological: its sub-title, *Poèmes de la paix et de la guerre (1913–1916)*, is both a note of the period of composition, as in *Alcools: Poèmes 1898–1913*, and an indication that the volume forms a direct sequel to the earlier one. But in addition the sub-title gives a definition of subject-matter: the collection is directly linked with external events of the period, notably the First World War, in which Apollinaire along with many other millions of men took part until he was invalided out in 1916. Such a shared experience helps avoid the private element of *Alcools*. Secondly the war imposes a thematic unity on most of the volume. To this Apollinaire adds a further unifying factor, brought forward from *Alcools*: his continued preoccupation with love. No longer is love lost through any fault of the poet's: now it is absent love that obsesses him. And as separation was forced upon him, he can understandably turn from amorous self-pity to erotic fantasies. The frustration of trench life for a man who so demonstrably (and demonstratively) needed the physical presence of women built up great pressures within him. But since, with considerable will-power, he refused to indulge in the self-abuse prevalent around him (there are some amusing accounts of masturbation sessions in the *Lettres à Lou*), the outlet for his passion was both an immersion in his job and the act of writing. There is, finally, greater stylistic unity than in *Alcools*, despite the appearance of the picture-poems, due partly to the shorter period covered, partly to his greater maturity and self-assurance and partly to the fact that at the front he had to be far more self-reliant. An impressionable person is influenced by things, people and events around him: for Apollinaire, 'la vraie vie' was elsewhere only in the superficial sense that he would rather have been in Paris than in the trenches. In no sense was

Apollinaire a metaphysical poet: he revelled in immediacy, and
that is both his main limitation and his main attraction.

Undoubtedly the most striking and disorientating feature of
Calligrammes is the inclusion of what Apollinaire at first called
'idéogrammes lyriques' and subsequently 'calligrammes', in
which his lyrical vision turned to visual lyricism (see illu-
stration). Defending the form against the adverse criticism of a
friend, André Billy, Apollinaire wrote:

> Note que je te trouve sévère pour les clichés. C'est un moyen moderne
> dont on aurait tort de se priver. C'est un premier livre de cette sorte et
> rien ne s'oppose à ce que, d'autres allant plus loin dans la perfection que
> moi qui ai commencé cette sorte de poésie, il n'y ait des livres calligram-
> matiques fort beaux un jour ... ils sont une idéalisation de la poésie
> vers-libriste et une précision typographique à l'époque où la typographie
> termine brillamment sa carrière, à l'aurore des moyens nouveaux de
> reproduction que sont le cinéma et le phonographe. (*O.C.*, iv, 778)

Billy was not convinced, continuing to call them some fifty years
later a 'voie sans issue'.[1] Apollinaire was more enthusiastic than
accurate in claiming to have invented the form. We know, for
example, that he had read and relished Rabelais and even
mentions (*O.C.*, ii, 723) the 'Dive bouteille' that figures as a
pictogram in *Le Cinq Livre* (chap. 44). It is unimaginable that he
had not come across Mallarmé's 'Un coup de dés jamais n'a-
bolira le hasard', first published in a periodical in 1897 and
separately in 1914. Even if he had not discovered English
examples (from Stephen Hawes to George Herbert, from George
Wither to Lewis Carroll) or some of the French 'Rhétoriqueurs',
it would be surprising if in his wide reading he had not come
across the *Greek Anthology* in which there are several examples of
early technopaignia (the Greek word for such picture-poems) by
Dosiadas, Simmias and others.

While we may readily dismiss Apollinaire's rash claim to
originality, and recognise that at best the form can be only a
byway of literature, it is worth reflecting further on the poet's
stimulating sense of the potential of an inter-generic approach to
art. From their very early days, he had an open mind about the
aesthetic possibilities of film and sound-recording. Similarly his
close involvement, as both journalist and friend, with the cubist
and simultanist painters of pre-war Paris led him to reflect,

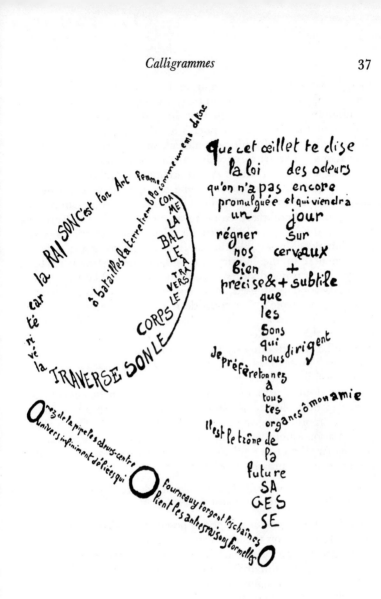

La Mandoline
l'œillet et le bambou

though more in practice than in theory, on the relationship between painting and literature. A logical counterpart to Apollinaire's syncretism, evident in 'Zone', 'La Chanson du mal-aimé' and many other poems in *Alcools*, is the challenge of simultaneity to a duration-bound art such as poetry. However long it may take us to perceive all the finer details of either a poem or a painting, there is a fundamental difference between the ways in which we first become acquainted with the work: one needs time to be read or heard whereas the other can be seen at a glance. Apollinaire came to an unsatisfactory compromise between the two media since his ideograms, 'privés de toute audition possible' as Billy noted (loc. cit.), also ignore a factor fundamental to the literary use of language, namely rhythm. They are amusing doodles. Apollinaire cannot take their visual aspect beyond a stylised representation of the object evoked, whereas Mallarmé's 'Un coup de dés' had already gone much further. Nor can he prevent the picture disappearing as we decipher the text. Nor, with rare exceptions, is the text *per se* paid sufficient attention by the poet to retain intrinsic interest as literature. Instead of bridging a gap successfully, the calligrammes fall between two stools.

Their double aim of surprise and simultaneity nonetheless allows of other forms of expression which are more satisfactory because more integrated, and the opening of the volume provides some notable examples. 'Liens', the first poem, may be seen as Apollinaire's equivalent to Rimbaud's vertiginous tight-rope dance in 'Phrases' (*Illuminations*):

J'ai tendu des cordes de clocher à clocher, des guirlandes de fenêtre à fenêtre, des chaînes d'or d'étoile à étoile, et je danse.

Each is a metaphor of the poet's power of analogy; each poises poetry delicately on the links thus made; each is the quintessence of an *art poétique*. Rimbaud's statement is more cryptic and multivalent; Apollinaire's more concerned with establishing the variety of possible connections and underlining the primacy of immediate sense perception in this process. Standing at the threshold of the volume, 'Liens' also assumes importance as a statement of certain aesthetic principles which, although present in *Alcools*, openly govern its sequel. The aesthetics of variety, incorporating the element of surprise, is bolstered by the suppression of obvious links in the interest of less apparent ones. Sense impressions of various types may therefore be juxtaposed, as in the opening line, set apart:

Cordes faites de cris

Not only does this seem to be a periphrasis for 'poems' (one thinks of Valéry's remark that poetry is a formalised verbal utterance of our 'cris'[2]), it also suggests and prepares us for a measure of discontinuity within a unit. Certain poems in *Alcools* written near the date of publication show this characteristic, as we have seen, but it comes to the fore in *Calligrammes* and is taken to further extremes.

In one respect, then, 'Liens' summarises the earlier volume; in another it seems specifically to repudiate it:

> *J'écris seulement pour vous exalter*
> *O sens ô sens chéris*
> *Ennemis du souvenir*
> *Ennemis du désir*
>
> *Ennemis du regret*
> *Ennemis des larmes*
> *Ennemis de tout ce que j'aime encore*
>
> (ll. 18–24)

Aware of his penchant for melancholy and regret for the past and his former loves, aware, in short, of the element of self-indulgence in the elegiac strain, Apollinaire now wants to explore the *hic et nunc* of the senses—not forgetting the 'quelques autres' beyond the normal five (see p. 26 above). 'Liens' thus presents a programme, quite specifically, for the first, 'pre-war' section, 'Ondes', as well as guiding the reader through *Calligrammes* to the *ars poetica atque humana* which closes the volume, 'La Jolie Rousse'. The last four poems of 'Ondes' ('Tour', 'Voyage', 'A travers l'Europe' and 'Il pleut') seem to enlarge on embryonic suggestions made verbally in 'Liens': 'Tours' (l. 12), 'Rails qui ligotez les nations' (l. 4), 'à travers l'Europe' (l. 2) and 'Violente pluie qui peigne les fumées' (l. 8). 'Tours' reappear in 'Les Fenêtres' (ll. 19, 20). For the 'Sons de cloches' (l. 2) we hear 'le son d'une flûte' as background music in 'Le Musicien de Saint-Merry' and there are 'd'autres liens plus ténus'. 'Araignées' (l. 13) recur in 'Les Fenêtres' (l. 12) and a train there links Vancouver with other towns. Ariadne appears three times in different guises (as 'la Taupe-Ariane' in 'Arbre', l. 19; twice, as herself and as a pastoral dancer, in 'Le Musicien de Saint-Merry', ll. 14, 67) to link the section together with her thread. If 'Liens' covers 'Câbles sous-marins' (l. 11) and 'Blancs rayons de lumière' (l. 16), 'Les Collines' can likewise stretch from 'le ciel splendide' (l. 163) 'jusqu'aux profondeurs incolores' (l. 155) and look forward to 'Le Musicien de Saint-Merry' ('c'est moi-même / Qui suis la flûte dont je joue', ll. 118–19) and to 'Sur les prophéties' ('Voici s'élever des prophètes', l. 56). All in all, there is evidence of close cross-referencing within the section which is further held together as a unit by the first poem. The fact that, in a volume where typography is so crucial, it is printed in italics suggests that Apollinaire wanted us to attach particular importance to it. Not only does it crystallise his aesthetic stance of the time; it also succeeds in its own right as a poem enacting that stance.

While it might also in passing be seen as a plea for under-standing at a time when war is approaching, a more fruitful question is: Who are the 'deux ou trois hommes / Libres de tous liens' (ll. 5–6)? The poet asks to join hands with them, suggesting a sense of affinity with fellow-artists who seem to be making similar experiments to his own, though in different media perhaps, and whose work might be made even more valuable for everyone by collaboration. Apollinaire was never one to make a secret of his—even provisional—discoveries, and expected and usually found the same openness in his friends. His preoccupation with painting made him at one stage consider the title *Et moi aussi je suis peintre* for a collection of his early calligrammes. A later chapter will present his relations with painters and writings on art more fully: for the moment it is enough to recall the principle of simultaneity practised first by the cubists and then, more grandly, by Robert Delaunay with whom Apollinaire became firm friends in 1913. If these painters were intent on introducing duration into their work, different views of the same object on one canvas implying different times of viewing, Apollinaire was no less intent on attempting to deny duration in poetry. Whereas the Symbolists' creed had been, in

Valéry's words, 'reprendre à la Musique leur bien', Apollinaire's quarry is not music but painting.

'J'aime beaucoup mes vers depuis *Alcools* ... et j'aime beaucoup beaucoup "Les Fenêtres" qui a paru à part en tête d'un catalogue du peintre Delaunay. Ils ressortissent à une esthétique tout neuve dont je n'ai plus depuis retrouvé les ressorts' (*O.C.*, iv, 493). 'Les Fenêtres' is certainly a succession of disparate remarks and references, and except in the memory is doomed to remain duration-bound; as Philippe Renaud writes, it is not a 'discours' but a 'parcours' (*Lecture d'Apollinaire*, p. 357). Yet Apollinaire's frequentation of Delaunay had made him ponder on the nature of the two-dimensional and its relation to time. If, towards the end of December 1913, he could quite reasonably assert: 'dans la peinture tout se présente à la fois, ... dans la littérature, dans la musique, tout se succède et l'on ne peut revenir sur tel mot, sur tel son au hasard' (*O.C.*, iv, 351), it suggests that Delaunay's 'simultanéisme' had stimulated him in various ways, not least as an impossible goal for a poet to try and reach. Insoluble problems are, after all, the only really interesting ones. Renaud is rash to dismiss as illusion (loc. cit.) the idea of simultaneity in this poem, the more so as it lies behind so many other poems in the volume including, of course, the calligrammes themselves. The challenge of simultaneity informs the section even if it necessarily remains an unrealisable dream.[3]

'Les Fenêtres' certainly has dream-like qualities: the reader is left to create his own links stimulated by ellipsis. The juxtapositions follow no rational pattern and colours kaleidoscope obsessively as a backdrop to the poet's record of random thoughts and observations. For it seems that this, like 'Arbre' and 'Lundi rue Christine' in the same section, is in part at least a 'poème-conversation', a text that notes as they occur fragments of conversation overheard from people around the poet. That it is more than this is evident from the evocation of 'pihis', the mythical one-winged bird that had figured in 'Zone', and from the verbal echoes within the poem (l. 35 repeats the first line; l. 11 is taken up in the penultimate line). And in various structuring ways, more or less obscurely, the poem seems to evoke the place-names listed towards the end: Paris at the outset; Vancouver from 'Et l'oie oua-oua trompette au nord' to

'Où le train blanc de neige ... fuit l'hiver'; Hyères in the
Mediterranean sea-food of line 17; Maintenon is less sure but
harks back to 'maintenant' (l. 11) and could evoke Madame de
Maintenon in the 'Beauté pâleur' (='Beauty parlour'?) of line
13; New York is physically represented sideways on the page in
its skyscrapers and gulf-like streets between:

> Tours
> Les Tours ce sont les rues
> Puits
> Puits ce sont les places
> Puits

(ll. 19–23)

and lastly the West Indies are present in lines 24–6, 'Câpresses'
and 'Chabin(e)s' being inhabitants of those islands. When, with
all this, one also has to encompass puns which proliferate on
closer inspection ('Hyères Maintenon' for 'hier maintenant';
'Quand on a le temps on a la liberté' suggesting two newspaper
titles; and as Renaud suggests, 'Paris Vancouver' for 'Paris:
vent, couvert', being a weather report for that city; 'et les
Antilles', according to him too, could be 'elle est gentille'
pronounced with a Caribbean 'zézaiement'; 'Puits' for 'puis';
'l'oie oua-oua' etc.), the text seems to add up to its sixth line: a
'Traumatisme géant'.

That humour, even the slightest of word-play, should be an
integral part of Apollinaire's most serious new experiment is both
infuriating and exciting. It necessarily frustrates the critic trying
to categorise his work and excites the reader who feels that since
everything is valid material for poetry humour has the right to
be included. While poetry, like a game (and Mallarmé called it
the 'Jeu suprême'), must be taken seriously for the best results,
there is every reason for it not to be a solemn and humourless
occupation despite a strong tradition inclining it that way.
Apollinaire was rarely solemn and played a major part in
putting the fun back in poetry: all the more reason why we
should remonstrate when he does take himself too seriously,
while acknowledging the ephemeral nature of much humour and
its possible consequent threat to poetry.

It is surely as fun, for instance, that we should take his next
text, 'Paysage', the first calligramme we come to in the book.

The landscape includes a house, a bush, a spread-eagled person or pair of lovers and a smoking cigar. They share an elliptical relationship and each sketchy shape is identified and defined by the meaning of the words it comprises. Just as in 'Les Fenêtres', sight and hearing are the senses involved, though in both texts the nose twitches at the end, there with the tang of an orange being opened and here with the whiff of cigar-smoke rising. It is a lightweight creation: we do not here find 'Toute l'âme résumée' as in Mallarmé's meditation of that title on smoking a cigar. Apollinaire would think it enough to have aroused our curiosity and either raised a smile or provoked antipathy for his legitimate experiment. So much of what he wrote was poetic journalism that he did not see lasting profundity as a necessary goal. There is room for a poet of inconsequentiality.

Which being established, Apollinaire, true to Protean form, plunges us headlong into the forty-five allegorical stanzas of 'Les Collines'. It is a somewhat laboured echo of Baudelaire's 'Les Phares' in that the hills of Apollinaire's poem are the peaks of human visionary achievement:

> Certains hommes sont des collines
> Qui s'élèvent d'entre les hommes
> Et voient au loin tout l'avenir
> Mieux que s'il était le présent
> Plus net que s'il était passé
>
> (ll. 26–30)

Implicitly, Apollinaire sees himself as one of the outstanding few: the 'je' of the poem predicts the birth of prediction (ll. 23–5) and stands poised between the future and a past which bears obvious autobiographical traces (e.g. ll. 101–10). The tussle between past and future—between order and adventure—is first seen as aerial combat, but this image is soon ousted by a *leitmotif* we have already seen connected with the magus: flames. Having attained 'la grâce ardente' (l. 126) and thereby the eternal present of artistic vision, the poet archly arrogates to himself the sole right to sing. His utter confusion about poetic means is evident in the lines:

> C'est de souffrance et de bonté
> Que sera faite la beauté

> Plus parfaite que n'était celle
> Qui venait des proportions
>> (ll. 171–4)

He admits further: 'J'écris ce que j'ai ressenti' (l. 177) as if this were sufficient for poetry. But if 'proportions' are a constricting risk to poetry, leading perhaps to empty versification, the spontaneous overflow of powerful emotion takes no account of forms of expression. A cry, a laugh is material for poetry, not a substitute for it. There is, however, room for surprising juxtapositions, and if this is what Apollinaire means, he gives some oneiric examples from stanza 37 on, surrealist *avant la lettre*. Where Lautréamont had on his poetic operating table an umbrella and a sewing machine (to the delight of André Breton and the surrealists), Apollinaire too has his still life take an eery turn:

> Un chapeau haut de forme est sur
> Une table chargée de fruits
> Les gants sont morts près d'une pomme
> Une dame se tord le cou
> Auprès d'un monsieur qui s'avale
>> (ll. 181–5)

The principle of arbitrary juxtaposition allows the active reader to make good the hiatus and imagine associations where none may exist. So 'Arbre' and 'Lundi rue Christine' make a virtue of random thoughts or snatches of conversation. The technique is a daring one, allowing the reader to play almost the same psychoanalytical game as the writer. Coherence is not sought: the aim is that something marvellous should happen to take us out of our everyday selves. Both 'Arbre' and 'Lundi rue Christine' could be café- and street-scenes, with 'la nostalgie d'un ailleurs' reminiscent of Larbaud (of whom the phrase was written) and Cendrars. Like 'Zone' (which also owes a debt to Cendrars in his 'Pâques à New-York') they have their partisans, notably among Parisian surrealists, who appreciate the fresh spontaneity evinced in an urban poetry prepared to concentrate on evanescent banalities. If they have 'ni queue ni tête', is it perhaps because Apollinaire is trying here to suggest a circularity of circumscription in which many voices speak simultaneously? However discursive, these poems could in yet another way be seeking to 'reprendre à la *peinture* leur bien', especially if one thinks of the dynamist and futurist paintings of the time, those, for example, by Delaunay and Boccioni. All in all the first section marks a clear advance on *Alcools* and shows Apollinaire still searching for a satisfactory aesthetic supple enough to embrace his many moods. The very last—near-vertical!—line of the section shows his continued preoccupation with what must be considered the principal *leitmotif* of 'Ondes', namely links:

écoute tomber les liens qui te retiennent en haut et en bas

('Il pleut')

*   *   *

No intrinsically different problems are raised by the other texts in 'Ondes', and pressure of space demands that we move on to the war poems. Although *Calligrammes* appeared only in March 1918, it will be recalled that the period covered by the volume is specified in the sub-title as 1913–1916. Only the last three poems in the book post-date Apollinaire's injury which occurred in March 1916, even if the incident provides a title for the final section, 'La Tête étoilée'. And only a relatively small number of poems, all in the last three sections, date from after 22 November 1915 when he transferred from the artillery to the infantry to obtain a commission (see *O.C.*, iv, 613): from external or internal evidence these seem to be 'Océan de terre', 'Aussi bien que les cigales', 'Du coton dans les oreilles', 'Le Vigneron champenois', 'Souvenirs', 'L'Avenir', 'Chant de l'honneur', 'Tristesse d'une étoile', 'La Victoire' and 'La Jolie Rousse'. The matter is of consequence since it shows that the bulk of Apollinaire's war-poems were written before the transfer, and as he declares in his first letter to Madeleine Pagès as a second lieutenant: 'un sous-off[icier] d'artillerie vit beaucoup plus confortablement à la guerre qu'un officier supérieur de fantassins' (*O.C.*, iv, 614). That turned out to be the most flagrant understatement. 'Maintenant c'est la guerre, pour de bon' (*O.C.*, iv, 616); '9 jours sans se laver, couché par terre, sans paille, sur un sol rempli de vermine, pas une goutte d'eau' (*O.C.*, iv, 618); 'Quelle effroyable boue dans les effroyables boyaux' (*O.C.*, iv, 628). The full horror of trench warfare at the front is brought home to him and it effectively silences the poet: 'En réalité, aucun écrivain ne pourra dire la simple horreur, la mystérieuse vie de la tranchée' (*O.C.*, iv, 621). What we have in the five war sections of *Calligrammes* is therefore an unbalanced picture: in spite of his avid quest for new experience, Apollinaire was certainly one of those who could not bear too much reality. For some writers knew that same front at first hand and wrote powerfully and movingly of its wasteful horrors: in English the greatest poetic monument to it is David Jones's *In Parenthesis*, but one also thinks of Owen, Rosenberg, Sassoon and Graves (the last two also in their memoirs). In French, I know of no poet of the First World War to match them, just as Henri Barbusse's *Le Feu* has no English counterpart.

The fact that the bulk of the war poems in *Calligrammes* were written when Apollinaire was in the artillery, at the front certainly but at a distance nonetheless from the unspeakable horror of the front-line trenches, goes some way to defending him against charges of inadequate moral and emotional responses. Marie-Jeanne Durry followed Breton and Aragon in pointing out the discrepancy between the cataclysmic situation and the slightness of Apollinaire's verbal reaction: 'Il faudrait plus que le déchirement mondial pour l'empêcher de jouer avec les mots!'[4] Unease about the discrepancy is understandable and proper, but Mme Durry is surely wrong in her analysis: it would not take *more* to stop Apollinaire playing with words, but *less*. Tension may be released in many ways, escapism take many forms. Humour for a poet seems to be a mechanism not simply of escapism but also of recognition of an ineffable inequality between his impotence *vis-à-vis* reality and his power over words. When he is more in control of a situation he is less prone to pun (and his calligrammes are visual-cum-verbal puns) and he loses his nervous twitch of humour. Yet under strain, it kept his spirits up and so helped him bolster the morale of his comrades-in-arms: by all accounts he was an excellent soldier from this point of view. We all have moral and emotional inadequacies: the war proved Apollinaire adaptable and resilient, able to give and receive orders without arrogance or subservience, a man of action not without reflection, and brimming with *camaraderie*. We should not impute personality deficiencies from our judgement that the poetry is inadequate to the occasion.

But in any case, was it? Are we not expecting of it something it never set out to achieve? And is word-play necessarily worse, or more false, than jingoism, sentimentalism, naturalism or other literary responses to the horrors of war? We cannot legitimately presuppose that any given response to war automatically generates good or bad poems, though we will most often tend to praise works that match our own prejudices. In fairness to Apollinaire we should try to see what he said and how he said it. If we discover inadequate *poetic* responses, then we may reasonably make an adverse judgement.

In his correspondence, Wilfred Owen recalls Vigny's observation: 'If any man despairs of becoming a poet, let him carry his pack and march in the ranks.'[5] Whether Apollinaire knew the original or not, he showed himself keen to join up although as a foreigner not obliged to do so. 'La Petite Auto' opens the second section of the volume, 'Etendards', and offers the first example of a calligramme inserted in a linear text. Most 'mixed' forms of this sort are in fact grouped in 'Etendards' and show Apollinaire experimenting further with the potential of ideographic elements. Within the narrative framework of a journey made in Rouveyre's car from Deauville to Paris, the sense of impending doom is presented as a catalyst to Apollinaire's awareness that things, and he with them, had changed, changed utterly:

Nous dîmes adieu à toute une époque

(l. 5)

Nous arrivâmes à Paris
Au moment où l'on affichait la mobilisation
Nous comprîmes mon camarade et moi
Que la petite auto nous avait conduits dans une époque Nouvelle
Et bien qu'étant déjà tous deux des hommes mûrs
Nous venions cependant de naître

(*in fine*)

Gigantic forces are sensed being unleashed around the frail automobile: there is here a keen sense of the discrepancy between three burst tyres and 'géants furieux', 'poissons voraces', between the serried silence of three anxious men (Apollinaire, Rouveyre and their chauffeur) and 'Océans profonds où remuaient les monstres', 'Hauteurs inimaginables' where airmen

fall like shooting stars. Men flock like sheep to the slaughter after
being drugged by the hollow rhetoric of politicians:

> Et des bergers gigantesques menaient
> De grands troupeaux muets qui broutaient les paroles
>
> (ll. 29–30)

Nothing here suggests inadequacy of response, and the visual
image of the little car making its tentative way through the dark
is fixed more clearly in the memory by the calligramme (even if
in some editions it is almost impossible to decipher). Apollinaire's sense of incorporating within himself 'toutes ces armées qui
se battaient' and the country in which they are fighting (ll. 12
ff.) allows an imaginative empathy made more possible by his
knowledge of the region, as the dialect word 'pouhons' underlines. The dogs of war are let slip in his mind and produce this
somewhat absolute but nonetheless effective allegory.

'Fumées', which incorporates the calligramme of a pipe, comes
to life only in the closing lines, particularly in the apposition of
'Ces nonchalantes femmes / Tes feuilles de papier' in which the
poet's love affair with his writing materials is succinctly conveyed. With the preceding composite calligramme 'La
Mandoline l'œillet et le bambou' (none of which is readily
recognisable as such), 'Fumées' seems to record Apollinaire's
pre-enlistment period at Nice when he smoked drugs. They do
not appear to have helped his poetry.

'A Nîmes' sees him in the army and provides the first example
of a notable feature of Apollinaire's war poems, namely the
erotic imagery intimately linked with aspects of warfare. Here
the tussle between passion and duty is shown first with the
elements separated and given a hemistich each (pale shades of
Corneille!), then fused in an image where duty itself is
passionate:

> L'Amour dit Reste ici Mais là-bas les obus
> Epousent ardemment et sans cesse les buts
>
> (ll. 5–6)

The poem's heroic couplets are generally trivialised not simply
because of humdrum references but more particularly because
the language is flaccid and the manner inconsequential.

'La Colombe poignardée et le jet d'eau' is the second and last composite calligramme in 'Etendards' and has an internal coherence which is twofold: it consistently regrets absent friends—girls in the dove, men in the fountain—and relates the two by having the dove fluttering near the fountain both in the text and on the printed page. Rhyme, and notably the insistent assonance of [i] in the dove, helps structure the calligramme further. It is most often alluded to, however, for the references in the text to Apollinaire's friends and to some suspicion of a guilty conscience at work: if Braque, Jacob and the others are fighting and perhaps even dying for their country why is Apollinaire not at the front?

By the next poem, he is. '2e canonnier conducteur' (Apollinaire's rank at the time) incorporates a number of ideographic elements, the first of which is an example of the 'canons–priapes' which fuse military and erotic elements. (The phrase 'ces canons ... sont de vigoureux priapes' occurs even before the war in *Le Poète assassiné*, *O.C.*, i, 242.) It did not of course take a war for Apollinaire to recognise the phallic form of a cannon, but it is another example of his close and persistent association of love and war which has led some critics to see him as heartless and cynical. The poem also contains a reference to the infantry which Apollinaire was later to join: it is a powerful and concise image of poor sods, vivid in its immediacy but with deep roots in archetypal, universal imagery:

> Voici des fantassins aux pas pesants aux pieds boueux
> La pluie les pique de ses aiguilles le sac les suit
> Fantassins
> Marchantes mottes de terre
> Vous êtes la puissance
> Du sol qui vous a faits
> Et c'est le sol qui va
> Lorsque vous avancez
>
> (ll. 10–17, discounting calligrammes)

And there is also the first instance of Apollinaire's reaction to the sheer spectacle of warfare, a thing which many of the writers of the period noted, though usually with a greater sense of unease than Apollinaire displays:

La Victoire se tient après nos jugulaires
...
Nos salves nos rafales sont ses cris de joie
Ses fleurs sont nos obus aux gerbes merveilleuses

(ll. 23–6)

There is, along with a childish faith in such a Victory personified, a child-like freshness of vision, unmindful of effect in real terms, concentrating its attention on the sensual impact of the instruments of death. Such unconcern with the lives at stake is not cynicism. Cynicism implies an awareness of the hurt as well as a disregard for it. Apollinaire seems rather not to have been aware of it yet: for all his affability in company he was enormously self-centred, and this might even be considered a necessary qualification for a lyric poet. He could easily persuade himself of the rightness of the French cause (the more so as a foreigner over-compensating for the fact) and feel his conscience free to let sensations overwhelm him. Alternatively, he might not have allowed himself to ponder too long on death and destruction: it would be one form of protection against emotional vulnerability simply to blot the thought out of his mind and accept what came to him. This again would not be callousness or cynicism but a valid recognition of both his own frailty and his salient passion for immediacy as opposed to any considered, long-term view. Regrettably this often led in his poetical writings to cheap, journalistic effects at the expense of more durable qualities.

'Case d'armons', the third section, originally 'jelligraphed' (that is, polycopied using a gelatine process) at the front, contains many slight pieces. It is here that he asserts, in 'Mutation':

Et tout
　　A tant changé
　　　　En moi
　　Tout
　　　　Sauf mon Amour
(ll. 12–16)

with which we can readily agree provided we understand by 'Amour' not steadfastness to a single woman but sentimental attachment to an ideal including a large dose of 'amour-propre'. A sense of constancy is nonetheless relevant to the poem in

another way: its 'Eh! Oh! Ha!' refrain contains an element of
irony, but more importantly it sets the other observations in the
timeless context of folk- and popular-song and so defuses the
situation of its horror:

> Une femme qui pleurait
> Eh! Oh! Ha!
> Des soldats qui passaient
> Eh! Oh! Ha!
> ...
> Des obus qui pétaient
> Eh! Oh! Ha!
> (ll. 1–4, 9–10)

Even the final 'Eh! Oh! Ha!' after 'Sauf mon Amour' gives a
last twist away from the particular circumstance to link the
claim of undying love to an infinity of such promises (with the
appropriate proportion of broken ones) throughout the ages of
soldiery.

Is it mere perversity that makes Apollinaire write in 'Oracles'
'O Guerre / Multiplication de l'amour' (ll. 9–10)? A close look
at one of the most famous of his war poems juxtaposing images of
love and war will indicate both how Apollinaire saw the relationship and how far this might be acceptable. I refer to 'Fête'
which also picks up the references to roses which appear insis-
tently in three of the poems which precede it: 'De la batterie de
tir', 'Echelon' and 'Vers le sud'. It also proceeds in a less direct
sense from the disenchantment generating a somewhat desperate
optimism that one finds in 'Toujours':

> Toujours
> Nous irons plus loin sans avancer jamais
> (ll. 1–2)

leads in the end to:

> Perdre
> Mais perdre vraiment
> Pour laisser place à la trouvaille
> Perdre
> La vie pour trouver la Victoire
> (ll. 13–17)

In 'Fête' spurious hope is death to the roses and there are

elements of wishful thinking; the disenchantment too remains, and the apparently superficial and verbally playful opening is given depth by the gradual interpenetration of hard and soft textures, of the military and the erotic, of physical flesh doomed to die yet prone to loving. The firework display of flares and shellburst is seen as 'charmant' because the poet links it with the insolent display of a woman's breasts which he imagines himself having revealed. There seems to be an almost wilful disregard of texture to the benefit of visual apprehension, and this is further underlined by a later image triggered off by the shape and texture of fading roses:

> Car une rose lui redit
> La molle courbe d'une hanche
>   (ll. 17–18)

This soft curvature is then transferred back to the night air stroked and streaked by flying shells which make of 'le mol / Parfum nocturne' pervading the loved one's bedroom 'un terrible alcool'. It is undoubtedly an attempt on Apollinaire's part to 'Mêler quelque grâce au courage' (l. 4). 'Grâce' for him implies firstly feminine charm, then roses in a rich poetic tradition (he mentions in line 15 the medieval Persian poet Saadi whose *Gulistan* 'Rosegarden' he clearly knew along, no doubt, with Marceline Desbordes-Valmore's best-known poem, 'Les Roses de Saadi'). Through it his indifference is shaken. 'Courage' evidently entails a stern sense of accepting the harshness of war: a sensitive man is asked to betray his nature by being under orders to kill even—perhaps especially—a rose. A poet can never be indifferent to anything or he may turn out an indifferent poet. So here Apollinaire, attentive to the possible ambiguities of ellipsis, ends the poem by fusing the two terms of his imagery in the phrase 'Mortification des roses', apparently in apposition to 'tu' in the preceding line. But 'tu' is both death and the image of his loved one: life and death are implicit in each other. And through this interplay, the capitalised 'IL SUT AIMER' presented as a desirable epitaph is double-edged. Not only is it something Apollinaire would dearly wish to be able to say and have said of himself but it is also a thing of the past, the past historic standing out like a tombstone in all the present tenses of the rest of the poem. It is a monument more to the certainty of death than to the groping uncertainties of love. If there is something distasteful about the poem it is this rather than cynicism. If there is something pathetic about it, it is the desperation to achieve a depth of lasting love beyond and against Apollinaire's nature.

A different kind of desperateness, and one which seems far less palatable, is expressed in Apollinaire's patriotism. In *Goodbye to All That*, Robert Graves convincingly suggests that traditional patriotism could no longer apply at the front in the Great War and that it was replaced by a sense of loyalty to one's immediate comrades in the battalion and to the exceptional no man's land of front-line warfare. The conditions were so unimaginable to those at home, the gap between the politicians' persuasive speeches and the reality so huge, that patriotism simply became redundant. This did not, of course, prevent soldiers dreaming of their homeland, but their dreams were modest, not grandiose, of green fields and wife and family, not of tub-thumping, flag-wagging, government-induced chauvinism. 'Dulce et decorum est pro patria mori' could only, as with Owen, assume an ironic dimension once the front was reached. Then the gulf between the individual sentient being or the evidence of thousands going as cannon-fodder and the jingoism of the nation's leaders became all too painfully obvious. Then the politicians' lies and incompetence spelt death and destruction. We can explain Apollinaire's heart-on-sleeve patriotism in two main ways: the first is that during his time in the artillery he was not at the front itself and so did not witness the full horror; the second that as France was his adopted country he felt drawn to out-French the French in patriotism. Yet it is difficult not to recoil with embarrassment when reading lines such as

> O Roses ô France
> Nous nous pâmons de volupté
> A ton cou penché vers l'Est
> ('De la batterie de tir', ll. 6–8)

Without benefit of irony, such jejune expressions of '*A*mour sacré am*our* de la *Patrie*' as Apollinaire calls it in the silly mish-mash of 'Venu de Dieuze' might charitably be suppressed.

On the other hand, the way in which irony can be used to

exorcise the anguish of a sensitive man's reaction to war may be seen in 'Les Saisons'. After the evocation of the good old days in the first verse, its opening hemistich is sufficient to act as a reminder at the start of each subsequent quatrain, where the subject shifts to the war. Yet 'C'était un temps béni' gradually invades the very sense of war itself by simple juxtaposition. And the refrain is neatly poised between a sing-song rhythm conjuring up *insouciance* and a sense which fits Guy (a projection of Gui[llaume] himself, of course) firmly in a war situation. At one and the same time, then, the past is coloured by the present and the present made more bearable by the past. A sense of change within continuity is entirely appropriate to the title which, in a very real way, the poem can be said to enact. Even the use of 'rimes embrassées' for the stanzas seems well suited for thoughts of love which, specified at the outset, continue even under fire in the shape of the rings lovingly polished from aluminium casings. From the misery of war Apollinaire salvages such scraps and with the counterpointing of irony can, as here, transform them into nicely poised poetry.

The last poem in 'Case d'armons', 'La Nuit d'avril 1915' seems to contain a number of eminently quotable fragments without adding up to a satisfactory whole. It opens on a festive spectacle:

> Le ciel est étoilé par les obus des Boches
> La forêt merveilleuse où je vis donne un bal

and continues with a statement of psychological interest:

> Un amour qui se meurt est plus doux que les autres
>   (l. 13)

The surrealistic image 'Il pleut mon âme il pleut mais il pleut des yeux morts' (l. 19) is all the more sickening because of its possible truth. But in general the relationship between images of love and war, in which all is proverbially fair, raises no further questions to those already considered.

One poem I have left aside however is 'Les Soupirs du servant de Dakar'. While it contains certain Apollinairean hallmarks ('ma sœur ... / Aux seins durs comme des obus', ll. 10–11; 'Une nuit de sorcellerie / Comme cette nuit-ci / Où tant d'affreux regards / Eclatent dans le ciel splendide', *in fine*) it is stylistically alone here, being presented as a Senegalese soldier's reflections on his African background and his present participation in the war in Europe. It shows a capacity for imaginative projection on Apollinaire's part which links up with his early awareness of African and Oceanian art (cf. the ending of 'Zone') and may also connect with Blaise Cendrars's interest in negro writing which led to his *Anthologie nègre* (1921). If it partakes of the stereotype, there are some nice touches, as in the character of the bishop ('Si doux si doux avec ma mère / De beurre de beurre avec ma sœur', ll. 36–7), the willingness of the French authorities to enlist the African ('Je ne sais pas mon âge / Mais au recrutement / On m'a donné vingt ans / Je suis soldat français on m'a blanchi d'un coup', ll. 51–4) and the falsely naive question stemming from the telling juxtaposition of two styles of warfare 'Pourquoi donc être blanc est-ce mieux qu'être noir' (l. 56). Apollinaire's abilities as raconteur and versifier find here a relatively undemanding but successful outlet.

'Lueurs des tirs' starts with a group of seven short pieces in octosyllabic quatrains and continues with loosely-textured descriptive pieces of little force. 'Océan de terre', written after Apollinaire's transfer to the infantry, closes the section with, as the title indicates, a pervasive image of the ubiquitous mud. Before that are some self-aware reflections, of little verbal but no small psychological interest, on his quasi-fabrication of a fiancée:

Je ne la connais par aucun sens
...
Existes-tu mon amour
Ou n'es-tu qu'une entité que j'ai créée sans le vouloir
Pour peupler la solitude
...
Je t'adore ô ma déesse exquise même si tu n'es que dans mon
     imagination

(‘Dans l'abri-caverne', *in fine*)

Words come to the fore, too much for some palates, in the quatrains and notably in 'Les Grenadines repentantes' where no less than three senses of the word 'grenade' occur in the poem's eight lines. Through that single word, incongruity is made metaphor. Some will appreciate the metaphor, others deplore the incongruity; none would deny the impact. Unease about

'L'Adieu du cavalier' is of a related but different order: the often-quoted opening line: 'Ah Dieu! que la guerre est jolie' is scarcely less often given a hasty redemption through irony by reference to the second verse, where the echoing 'Adieu!' preludes a casual death. The case would be more convincing if one did not find in Apollinaire's letters unequivocal statements like 'La guerre est une chose charmante' (*O.C.*, iv, 917) until the fateful day in November 1915 when he changed arms. Referential confusion within the poem obscures its meaning: if the 'vous' behind 'vos soupirs' (l. 4) is also the 'elle' of line 7, how does one explain the shift from sighs of sympathetic longing to heartless laughter at death? If the 'vous' and 'elle' are different, who are they? If the former is Madeleine Pagès, could the latter be Marie Laurencin to whom the group of quatrain poems was sent under the title *Le Médaillon toujours fermé*? For she had twisted the knife in Apollinaire's wound by marrying a German not long after she had left him. If so, the oblique and private (and unjust) taunt might help explicate but scarcely benefits the poem. The suspicion remains that Apollinaire was interrupted after the first verse had been written and had other preoccupations by the time he came to write the second.

'Obus couleur de lune', the fifth section, contains more ambitious and interesting pieces. Only its two calligrammatic texts, 'Aussi bien que les cigales' and 'Du coton dans les oreilles' postdate Apollinaire's transfer, the latter closing the section on the words 'La vague / Dans les caves / Dans les caves', expressive both of the 'océan de terre' and of the subterranean quality of life in the trenches (and in the cellars of Champagne where Apollinaire was fighting). The section is interesting rather for further and different attempts at, as one of the titles has it, 'Simultanéités'. 'Merveille de la guerre', 'Il y a' and 'Simultanéités' itself seem to be various explorations of the impossibility of poetry withdrawing from duration. The first is the most conventional but perhaps the most rewarding. Apollinaire sees himself as the still centre of the turning world, all-pervading yet contained, plural yet singular. The single place is also the single moment which while expanding to embrace an infinity of events does not itself explode. The microcosmic is seen in macrocosmic terms, the pupil dilates:

... les chevelures sont devenues des comètes
Ces danseuses surdorées appartiennent à tous les
    temps et à toutes les races
...
C'est un banquet que s'offre la terre
...
Mais le festin serait plus beau encore si le ciel
    y mangeait avec la terre
...
J'ai creusé le lit où je coule en me ramifiant en
    mille petits fleuves qui vont partout
Je suis dans la tranchée de première ligne et cependant
    je suis partout ...
                              (ll. 5–6, 15, 21, 27–8)

The poem ends with one of those proud claims and calls to posterity that lyric poets feel entitled to make; fortunately this includes a caveat:

Je lègue à l'avenir l'histoire de Guillaume Apollinaire
Qui fut à la guerre et sut être partout
...
Et ce serait sans doute bien plus beau
Si je pouvais supposer que toutes ces choses dans
    lesquelles je suis partout
Pouvaient m'occuper aussi
Mais dans ce sens il n'y a rien de fait
Car si je suis partout à cette heure il n'y a cependant
    que moi qui suis en moi
                              (ll. 31–2, 39–43)

All the poetry is in the vision, none in the language; the eternal present is here a philosophical concept rather than a poetic reality.

'Il y a' goes some way to restoring the balance by the rudimentary technique of repetition: the title phrase opens all but the last two lines of the poem, though the variant 'Il y avait' also occurs once. Borrowed perhaps from the third part of 'Enfance' in Rimbaud's *Illuminations*, the feature occurs elsewhere in Apollinaire's work (cf. *O.C.*, iii, 375–6) to somewhat different effect. Here the succession of statements, not being sequential, suggests a kind of pivoting simultaneity where the fixed point is the poet's mind imprinted both with the marks of memory and with the evidence of perception. In this respect its attempt at both succession and simultaneity is like 'Les Fenêtres'. While it is a compromise between sequence and stasis and so inevitably precarious, the structure of 'Il y a' is more than usually firm. One knows from Baudelaire and Rimbaud, not to mention Racine, the importance of last lines and even last words. 'L'art de l'invisibilité' which closes 'Il y a' is the king-pin linking the two areas of reference in the text: love is invisible through physical separation, war both requires invisibility to improve chances of survival and imposes the invisibility of death. Posited in each of the first two lines, related in the third and thereafter pursued as interleaved topics, the poles of love and war are once again explored in their poignant relationship. Differently again, 'Simultanéités' probes their interaction, but no structural or syntactic element helps bear out the promise of the title beyond the juxtaposition of observations drawn from two areas. Again the poet's mind is the point of unity and this assertion of presence tallies well with Apollinaire's alert but self-centred involvement with immediacy.

As has been noted, seven of the thirteen poems in the final section, 'La Tête étoilée', are known to have been written after Apollinaire's transfer to the real front with the infantry. The last three in the book post-date his injury. In the others there is a marked return to a tone of autumnal melancholy reminiscent of *Alcools*, and there seems some tired wistfulness in 'Le Départ', 'Carte postale' and 'Un oiseau chante'. The one picture-poem, 'Eventail des saveurs', is too slight to redeem this, and it is left to the love poems of wishful thinking to inject some life—albeit a future, imaginary life—into the lassitude. 'Chevaux de frise' offers some refreshing visual imagery and verbal forms neatly underlining the poet's death-in-life situation:

> [La neige] toisonne d'hermine les chevaux de frise
> ...
> Chevaux muets
> Non chevaux barbes mais barbelés
>
> (ll. 15, 18–19)

Revivified by his imagination, the white horses in turn become waves bearing the poet's love across the Mediterranean: after

Alcools where love was here but not now, we see that in the war poems of *Calligrammes* love is now but not here. While we can scarcely help but sympathise, the frustrated emotion of the insistent 'Je t'aime' is not enough to transform it into poetry: indeed it becomes the inarticulate stutter that is all most of us can manage when feelings outrun our capacity for expressing them.

The rallying-cry of 'Chant de l'honneur' is a conscious turning away from the mud and misery of the front-line trenches. Written in the same month as 'Océan de terre', December 1915, it refuses to indulge in the sea-change which has overtaken the earth; where, in 'Océan de terre',

> Les poulpes terrestres palpitent
> Et puis nous sommes tant et tant à être nos propres fossoyeurs
> Pâles poulpes des vagues crayeuses ô poulpes aux becs pâles
>
> (ll. 14–16)

Apollinaire braces himself in 'Chant de l'honneur' to go beyond the evidence of his senses:

> J'ai plus que les trois cœurs des poulpes pour souffrir
> Vos cœurs sont tous en moi je sens chaque blessure
> O mes soldats souffrants ô blessés à mourir
>
> (ll. 22–4)

Through such sympathy *à la* Whitman (with the very varied reactions it is bound to provoke in readers), Apollinaire determines to see beauty in spite of everything. The result is a rather embarrassing dialogue between the poet, the trench, the bullets and France. Capital letters given to varieties of 'a Good Thing' (the terminology of *1066 and All That* seems singularly apposite here)—Amour, Beauté, Grâce, Vertu, Courage, Honneur, Gloire, Perfection, Victoire, Devoir—are relieved only by being applied also to 'Démangeaison', doubtless the most prevalent of them all. Again one would not wish to quarrel with the sentiments but with their expression, an insufficiency which Apollinaire seems to acknowledge in the penultimate line of the following passage which closes the poem:

> Prends mes vers ô ma France Avenir Multitude
> Chantez ce que je chante un chant pur le prélude
> Des chants sacrés que la beauté de notre temps

Saura vous inspirer plus purs plus éclatants
Que ceux que je m'efforce à moduler ce soir
En l'honneur de l'Honneur la beauté du Devoir

Does morale-boosting have to be so laboured to be effective? Has Apollinaire forgotten Vigny's clear priority: 'Ce qu'il y a de plus beau après l'inspiration, c'est le dévouement; après le Poète, c'est le Soldat'?[6] It seems that Apollinaire ignored the fact that propaganda and poetry are almost impossible to reconcile.

The small-scale, tightly-ordered poem 'L'Avenir' (dating from March 1916 only a few days before his injury) effectively dispels the hollow appeal to the future in 'Chant de l'honneur' where Apollinaire had written but not followed through his recognition that 'la beauté / N'est la plupart du temps que la simplicité' (ll. 10–11). Frail, fleeting things—snow, bee and rose—are equated with hands and thence with the future which is so elusive that the poet recommends: 'ne songeons pas à l'avenir' (l. 12). The brevity of the basic line (established as five syllables—a Verlainean 'impair'—but flexed from four even to twelve on one occasion) matches the evanescent quality of the evocation. The restrained, quiet tone reveals Apollinaire's most attractive poetic voice and achieves the eternal present with apparently effortless ease, a living proof that muscular contraction should not be confused with real concentration.

'Tristesse d'une étoile' records the injury to Apollinaire's head by a shell-splinter, puts the inside of his skull on a cosmic scale and insists that such physical suffering is as nothing compared with 'le secret malheur qui nourrit mon délire' (l. 7). What 'cette ardente souffrance' (l. 9) may be is not specified but it infects his whole being and is clearly ineffable. After such an experience, 'La Victoire' takes a surprising turn. Where from the title one might have expected something in the vein of 'Chant de l'honneur', it proves to be not an exercise in jingoism but an articulate plea for a fresh vision and more specifically a fresh language in which to express it. It could not unreasonably be read as a programme for Dada, and a sentence from *Le Poète assassiné* is worth recalling: 'Je n'écrirai plus qu'une poésie libre de toute entrave, serait-ce celle du langage' (*O.C.*, i, 257). Here at last is the fundamental reason behind all the experimentation of *Calligrammes*:

Remuons la langue

…

On veut de nouveaux sons de nouveaux sons de nouveaux sons
On veut des consonnes sans voyelles

…

Laisser pétiller un son nasal et continu
Faites claquer votre langue

…

Les divers pets labiaux rendraient aussi vos discours claironnants
Habituez-vous à roter à volonté

(ll. 30, 32–3. 36–7, 40–1)

Uncouthness is a necessary part of such a revolution close to anarchy, but an ingredient of such an almost Rabelaisian recipe is laughter:

Ce rire se répand
Partout

(ll. 57–8)

Apollinaire's preparedness to continue experimenting, searching even at the cost of being considered 'un hulerberlu' by detractors, is indicative both of laudable dissatisfaction and aesthetic insecurity. His projection towards the future at the end of 'La Victoire' heralds the last poem in the book:

La Victoire avant tout sera
De bien voir au loin
De tout voir
De près
Et que tout ait un nom nouveau

'La Jolie Rousse' ascertains and asserts Apollinaire's position as a pioneer, an adventurer teetering on the brink of the unknown, and asks for understanding and indulgence. Presenting a summary of his present state by reference to past actions, it stands as a pendant and a development of the aesthetic stance of 'Liens' and claims the poet's right and furthermore his ability to probe unspecified mysteries lying beyond the ordered world of tradition and reality:

Soyez indulgents quand vous nous comparez
A ceux qui furent la perfection de l'ordre
Nous qui quêtons partout l'aventure

Nous ne sommes pas vos ennemis
Nous voulons nous donner de vastes et d'étranges domaines
Où le mystère en fleurs s'offre à qui veut le cueillir
...
Pitié pour nous qui combattons toujours aux frontières
De l'illimité et de l'avenir

(ll. 17–22, 28–9)

Reason, so long the goddess of French culture, becomes 'la Raison ardente' figured by the auburn girl of the title (in real life Jacqueline Kolb, it appears, whom Apollinaire was to marry in 1918). The closing lines are both pathetic and triumphant:

Mais riez riez de moi
Hommes de partout surtout gens d'ici
Car il y a tant de choses que je n'ose vous dire
Tant de choses que vous ne me laisseriez pas dire
Ayez pitié de moi

Pressures from both within and without make him painfully conscious of his pivotal position between Order and Adventure, and here, though evidently with regret and no little nostalgia, he chooses the latter. It is certainly appropriate as an end for a volume which displays much formal experimentation but preserves both the viewpoint and many topics of traditional lyricism. The poet's restless eye revels in and records its immediate perceptions: we appreciate its bright alertness, its rejection of cant and preconceptions, the heart-on-sleeve sincerity of its vision, the novelty of some of its findings. The man behind the poetry enlists our attention and sympathy. But does his poetry? Does mediate language play a sufficient part in the literary artefact that he creates? Can his claim to special powers be supported by the poetry *qua* poetry and not simply spuriously dinned home by repetition? Only seldom, very seldom, does the answer seem to be in the affirmative. Too often the journalistic streak is uppermost; too often neither form nor texture draws attention to itself away from self-indulgence. *Calligrammes*'s relative unity of subject therefore puts it at a disadvantage compared with the variety of *Alcools*, and the unsureness of aesthetic stance throughout leads the bulk of the poems precariously near inarticulateness. Thematic studies prove psychological rather than poetic preoccupations and do not directly help to define value judgements. Nor do exciting individual lines or images of themselves redeem prosaic gangue. Apollinaire spells out his own failure in *La Femme assise*:

Douce poésie! je regrette que l'incertitude des temps ne me permette pas de me livrer à tes inspirations touchant la matière de ce livre, mais la guerre continue. Il s'agit, avant d'y retourner, d'achever cet ouvrage et la prose est ce qui convient le mieux à ma hâte. (*O.C.*, i, 372)

Fortunately whole gems are there for the finding, and it is ironic that they shine with an entirely traditional gleam.

IV

'LE BESTIAIRE' AND OTHER POEMS

Apart from the poems collected in *Alcools* and *Calligrammes*, Apollinaire published two slim volumes of verse during his lifetime, *Le Bestiaire ou Cortège d'Orphée* (1911) and *Vitam impendere amori* (1917). The first incorporates woodcuts by Raoul Dufy and the second line drawings by André Rouveyre. Otherwise, all the collections of poems were gathered and published posthumously with titles chosen by their editors: *Il y a* (1925), *Ombre de mon amour* (1947)—to become *Poèmes à Lou* in 1955—and *Le Guetteur mélancolique* (1952). The *Œuvres poétiques* in the Bibliothèque de la Pléiade also group the 'Poèmes à Madeleine' and 'Poèmes à la marraine', taken from Apollinaire's letters to Madeleine Pagès and Jeanne-Yves Blanc respectively, and add 'Poèmes retrouvés', 'Poèmes épistolaires' and 'Poèmes inédits' for good measure. Since I am not devoting a special chapter to Apollinaire's correspondence but using it as a source of reference throughout, I shall facilitate matters by referring to the Pléiade edition (as *O.P.*) in this chapter.

Le Bestiaire ou Cortège d'Orphée is a *divertissement* presenting in pithy verses the poet's claim to special powers through his place in the Orphic tradition. Frequent reference to Greek mythology is tied in with a delicious (sometimes malicious) sense of humour using the animals of the bestiary as a vehicle for comment on humans. A number of Apollinairean themes and features are adumbrated: metamorphoses created by the magus, syncretism, travelling, past and fleeting time, the difficulty of living, pride in poetry, the importance of the presence of friends and the pleasures of carnal love. One feature not to reappear in any but a thoroughly modified form is the apparently unquestioning acceptance of Christian terminology: we are invited to listen not to sirens but to 'les Anges du paradis' (*O.P.*, 26), to appreciate 'Ce beau poisson divin qu'est JESUS, Mon Sauveur' (*O.P.*, 20) and to have the message of the last poem in the sequence, 'Le Bœuf' (*O.P.*, 32), linger in our minds:

> Ce chérubin dit la louange
> Du paradis, où, près des anges,
> Nous revivrons, mes chers amis,
> Quand le bon Dieu l'aura permis.

Apollinaire's notes to the poems continue this attitude while explaining obscure references: 'Ceux qui s'exercent à la poésie ne recherchent et n'aiment rien autre que la perfection qui est Dieu lui-même' (*O.P.*, 35). With the passage of time, Apollinaire transfers his allegiance and piety to Orpheus but because of his equation of Orpheus and Christ (see 'Orphée', *O.P.*, 20) the transition may be considered innocent of specific hostility towards Christianity. Apollinaire made a religion of poetry in true nineteenth-century manner.

A partial, deprecating self-portrait is presented in 'Le Poulpe' (*O.P.*, 22):

> Jetant son encre vers les cieux,
> Suçant le sang de ce qu'il aime
> Et le trouvant délicieux,
> Ce monstre inhumain, c'est moi-même.

In 'La Souris' (*O.P.*, 13), he exclaims: 'Dieu! Je vais avoir vingt-huit ans, / Et mal vécus'. Such self-questioning carries its own appeal, counteracting the poet's obvious pride (perhaps too often affirmed) in his art: he has no need to fish for compliments, and the most charming poems are those where lightness of touch avoids any hint of cleverness and too much self-consciousness, for instance 'Le Chat', 'Le Dromadaire' and 'Le Paon'.

> Je souhaite dans ma maison:
> Une femme ayant sa raison,
> Un chat passant parmi les livres,
> Des amis en toute saison
> Sans lesquels je ne peux pas vivre.
>
> (*O.P.*, 8)

> Avec ses quatre dromadaires
> Don Pedro d'Alfaroubeira
> Courut le monde et l'admira.
> Il fit ce que je voudrais faire
> Si j'avais quatre dromadaires.
>
> (*O.P.*, 12)

> En faisant la roue, cet oiseau,
> Dont le pennage traîne à terre,
> Apparaît encore plus beau,
> Mais se découvre le derrière.
>
> (*O.P.*, 29)

Vitam impendere amori groups six brief poems written in octosyllabic quatrains on the topic of time and love gone by. Strictly limited to the tone of regret and self-pity they never catch fire: the images remain too general to be personalised and the language is unexciting. The pastel shades of memory colour 'le dernier des phénix' (*O.P.*, 158) and are not given the prospect of revitalisation enjoyed by the seasons. There are some points and counterpoints of rhythmic interest but if one compares a verse from the last poem with one of Rimbaud's one sees and hears immediately how dull Apollinaire is by comparison:

> O ma jeunesse abandonnée
> Comme une guirlande fanée
> Voici que s'en vient la saison
> Et des dédains et du soupçon
>
> (*O.P.*, 162)

> Oisive jeunesse
> A tout asservie,
> Par délicatesse
> J'ai perdu ma vie.
> ('Chanson de la plus haute tour')

Rimbaud is here spring-heeled, Apollinaire leaden.

The heteroclite collection entitled *Il y a* contains 'Les Dicts d'amour à Linda' and a number of other early pieces, three poems which Apollinaire published under his temporary female pseudonym Louise Lalanne and other texts in verse and prose culled from periodicals by the original editor of the volume, Jean Royère. As would be expected, the collection is very uneven: it includes, after all, material which Apollinaire had chosen not to publish in *Alcools*. The early pieces show elements of pastiche and are also traditional technical exercises in stanzaic form and borrowed voice, mixing elegant if slight conceits to sing the lady's praises. A cavalier approach to the alexandrine is already in evidence, and lessons in *enjambement* have clearly been learnt from the Symbolists. Yet at root it is the Renaissance that pervades these early works, and it is interesting to reflect that even in 'Per te praesentit aruspex' which first appeared with 'Le Pont Mirabeau' in *Les Soirées de Paris* in February 1912 one hears the shade of Ronsard celebrating another love affair or the ghost of Du Bellay, sad and sardonic as ever. The later poems mostly evoke places or people without adding resonances to those familiar from *Alcools* and *Calligrammes*; they are loose-textured, largely circumstantial, and memorable only when humour, irony or concision comes into play, for those qualities bring a lightness of touch or tone which strains neither poet nor reader and seems to characterise the former's dominant key. The brief, singing refrain in 'Le Souvenir du douanier',

> Je tourne vire
> Phare affolé
> Mon beau navire
> S'est en allé
> (*O.P.*, 357–9)

the playful irony of 'Avant le cinéma', the terse simplicity of 'Un poème' (allowing concentration on the juxtaposition of match and fire-extinguisher), the unembroidered emptiness of 'La Grenouillère' deserted by the Impressionist painters (whose female subjects are nicely if roguishly caught in 'des femmes à grosse poitrine / Et bêtes comme chou'): these are worth more than reams of self-indulgence and flaccidity, however picturesque these sometimes are.

Poèmes à Lou collects the verse and calligrammes from Apollinaire's letters to Louise de Coligny-Châtillon. Mainly love poems and information about the war and Apollinaire's state of mind, some of them were used directly or with some modification in *Calligrammes* while others are still considered too scabrous or indelicate for publication. Among the 'blasons du corps féminin', the related images of love and war, the private allusions, the confessional outpourings, the romantic musings, the amorous protestations, the excruciating puns, the rambling verses, the dross of unlicked epistolary discourse, the unstable moodiness, one finds few memorable pieces. The best certainly figure either unchanged or, as in the case of 'Les Saisons' and 'Fête', improved in *Calligrammes*. Accusations of insensitivity such as have already been discussed arise over lines such as 'Nos 75 sont gracieux comme ton corps' (*O.P.*, 380), 'Les canons membres génitaux / Engrossent l'amoureuse terre / ... / Pareille à l'amour est la guerre' (p. 407), 'Et j'écoute ... / Les obus s'envoler comme l'amour lui-même' (p. 430) or 'Deux fusants rose éclatement / Comme deux seins que l'on dégrafe' (p. 500, cf. 'Fête', p. 238). Petrarchan paradox ('the icy fire') is not explored beyond the straight comparison. Apollinaire's preparedness to accept and reiterate much that is traditional in poetry includes subject-matter that is normally winnowed from 'respectable' anthologies and collections. But herein lies one of his undoubted legacies: he did not draw a dividing-line between what was conventionally respectable and what lay beyond that pale. The most important canon he exploded, often with a great deal of smoke and noise, was that of good taste.

Examples can of course be found in *Alcools* and *Calligrammes* but they are even more patent in *Poèmes à Lou*. One reason for this is that they were never all meant for publication (Apollinaire envisaged printing only a discreet selection) but as part of an intimate correspondence, a factor also going some way to explaining their discursive qualities. The Renaissance tradition of emblematic verses in praise of each part of the beloved's body is used in various ways. 'En allant chercher des obus' (*O.P.*, 459–62) explores the body's nine orifices with candid interest; the poem beginning 'Mon très cher petit Lou je t'aime' (*O.P.*, 427–8) lists all Lou's erogenous zones and sensual attributes from her 'Vulve qui serre comme un casse-noisette' to her 'Démarche onduleuse et dansante'; deviations referred to are many and colourful. Yet a soldier's erotic recollections and fantasies would not be enough to undermine norms of respectability: both have existed side by side for thousands of years without insidious effect in either direction. More disturbing to taste than incongruity is illogicality and the complaisance of wilful self-delusion such as one finds in 'Parce que tu m'as parlé de vice ...' (*O.P.*, 396–7). The double standards are evident from the following extract:

Nous pouvons faire agir l'imagination
Faire danser nos sens sur les débris du monde

Nous énerver jusqu'à l'exaspération
Ou vautrer nos deux corps dans une fange immonde

...

Nous pouvons appeler soir ce qu'on dit matin

...

Je peux me prosterner comme vers un autel
Devant ta croupe qu'ensanglantera ma rage
Nos amours resteront pures comme un beau ciel

...

Le vice en tout cela n'est qu'une illusion
Qui ne trompe jamais que les âmes vulgaires

My criticism is not a moralising one: a broad- or narrow-minded stance is irrelevant to the condemnation of logic which is not only false (as memorably shown in Humpty-Dumpty's use of language in *Alice's Adventures in Wonderland*) but positively dangerous (as the twentieth century has learned at great cost from propagandists). The question-begging line 'Le vice n'entre pas dans les amours sublimes' shows just what a selfish, spoilt child Apollinaire could sometimes be.

If little in *Poèmes à Lou* is edifying, some of the poems are nonetheless moving. In 'Si je mourais là-bas . . .' (*O.P.*, 392-3), Apollinaire casts a disabused glance at his relationship with Lou and considers the eventuality of his death at the front. He predicts that she will find evidence of his existence all around her: his blood would colour everything from the sun to her nipples even though he may be nothing but a 'souvenir oublié'. Such self-detachment makes a welcome change in so much uncritical self-involvement. The unadorned terseness of 'Sonnet du huit février 191[5]' (*O.P.*, 408) guards against self-indulgence and matches the clipped irony which seems to be attached to everything and everybody—Lou, an Austrian soldier, hope and self—once Lou's indifference is clear: 'elle s'en fiche'.

The epistolary *ménage à trois* between Apollinaire, Lou and 'Toutou', Apollinaire's successful rival of the time, gives rise to some extraordinary psychological postures on the poet's part (he wants to have his cake and eat it yet again, encouraging Toutou while rebuking Lou for infidelity and wanting them both to love him) and some contrivedly funny fables. Playing on the words 'gui', 'loup' and 'toutou' (the last being a colloquial word for dog), Apollinaire contorts his frustrated urges into such attitudes as:

> Mais je n'en suis pas jaloux
> Les toutous n'font pas mal aux loups
>
> (*O.P.*, 490)

> Le toutou pour sa part eut bien plus (à tout prendre)
> De baisers que le gui
> Qui tout alangui
> Entre deux jolis seins ne peut rien entreprendre
> Mais se contente bien ma foi
> De son trône digne d'un roi
>
> (*O.P.*, 494)

The fable form, with La Fontaine's *vers libres*, is neatly handled and the moral invariably non-committal and humorous. Yet if Apollinaire reaches his target it is sad to have to admit that it is because he has set his sights low. He may nonetheless be given credit above less discriminating editors for having recognised that not all his verse was worthy of publication.

Le Guetteur mélancolique assembles poems written during or around the time of Apollinaire's stay at Stavelot in 1899, a group of 'Rhénanes' dating, like those in *Alcools*, from 1901–2 when he was employed by Countess von Milhau, five 'Poèmes à Yvonne' written for a neighbour who in 1903 aroused the poet's passing interest, and various pieces written over the whole of Apollinaire's creative life. While the juvenilia are of interest for those wishing to follow the poet's development, the 'Rhénanes' were by and large rightly excluded from *Alcools* for which many of the 'Poèmes divers' were also pillaged before being discarded.

A number of the Stavelot poems are simply the apprentice poet's five finger exercises, but in many cases the accents of the later Apollinaire can already be heard. His first lament at infidelity may be heard in the *quintil*:

> S'en est allée l'amante
> Au village voisin malgré la pluie
> Sans son amant s'en est allée l'amante
> Pour danser avec un autre que lui
> Les femmes mentent mentent
>
> (*O.P.*, 511)

His interest in languages and delight in playing with words and unashamed use of vulgarity are evident in 'Le Ciel se couvre un matin de mai'; the word 'ombraculifères' appears and then the earth is evoked:

> En latin c'est terra l'Allemand l'appelle Erde
> Un clair écho peut-être a su répondre Merde
>
> (*O.P.*, 521)

Colloquial and dialect forms occur elsewhere and indicate a good ear and a talent for mimicry which will never be lost. In the 'Rhénanes' occasional German words join the many proper nouns evoking the local scenes and suggest not only Apollinaire's relish for language but also his readiness to assert the value of fortuitous personal experience against the usual demands of easy communication. This too, as we have seen, was to remain an ironic feature at the heart of Apollinaire's poetry, yet it is interesting to see him scavenging among his early work for lines to incorporate in new and more richly communicative settings. From 'La Clef', for instance (*O.P.*, 553–5), were taken elements for three separate poems published in *Alcools* ('L'Adieu', 'Rhénane d'automne' and 'La Dame'), and parts of 'Le Printemps' (pp. 556–9) were re-used in 'L'Emigrant de Landor Road', 'Le Brasier' and 'Les Fiançailles'. Such self-pillaging is even more legitimate, of course, and less open to adverse criticism, than borrowing from others: it shows continuity of interests, tone and purpose in an *œuvre* which may in certain lights seem pathologically fragmented.

If the other three hundred pages of poems in the Pléiade volume are not presented here in detail it is not simply because they are less good than the work Apollinaire chose to publish in collections in his lifetime but because they would prompt only a rehearsal of the same critical problems as have already been raised. Many of the pieces shed light on aspects of the poet's biography, both external and intellectual; many offer interesting comparisons with the collected work. But if one compares, by way of example, the epistolary verses sent to Apollinaire's numerous correspondents—Salmon, Billy, Rouveyre, Lou, Madeleine etc.—with the poems, collected in *Calligrammes* for instance, which had originally figured as inserts in such letters, the qualitative difference is marked. In the former, the logic of discursive prose guides the writer through his able versification in a manner reminiscent of eighteenth-century wit. In the latter, the prime element of organisation is no longer open-ended but, through image structure or linguistic texture, self-regarding. The early calligramme 'Lettre-océan' is as clear an example of this, notably in its pictorial transmitting image, as such war poems as 'Fête' or 'Tourbillon de mouches', where a gain in tension is a gain for poetry.

Two conclusions derive from an inspection of Apollinaire's minor poetical works. The first is a confirmation of the variability of his aesthetic position, though this is more understandable and pardonable in juvenilia and slight pieces than in mature works. This variability is always linked to individual and idiosyncratic experience, so making the poetry run the risk of failure to communicate by the private nature of its referential area and by its explicit or implicit reliance on external evidence. Our judgement is inevitably complex if a poem written, let us say, for Lou, 'meant' more to Lou than it 'means' for us. For although the poem may fail the durability test, we must nonetheless concede its relative effectiveness in a particular situation: the line between *vers de circonstance* and great poetry stemming no less from human contingencies is a difficult one to draw. Intention is no guide; effect is notoriously volatile and subjective. And each shifts the centre of attention away from the written text. Intuitively, Apollinaire sensed this, for our second conclusion is that he showed himself far more judicious than his followers in the choice of what he published and collected. This conclusion should not be taken as ingratitude for the work of scholars but as recognition that no editor is likely to be so much a poet as Apollinaire himself.

V

PROSE AND PLAYS

Reverting to the *Œuvres complètes* as our basic source of reference, we turn our attention now to Apollinaire as prose writer and dramatist. In both fields he nonetheless remained very much the poet in so far as he continued to show an active interest in the obscurer byways of language and continued to attitudinise, as if anything goes once the label 'Poète: appellation contrôlée' has been stuck on. Beyond a certain amount of posturing, however, we find not only an agreeable companion but an accomplished raconteur. The easy-going charm suggested by a title such as *Le Flâneur des deux rives*, a collection of relaxed anecdotal tales of odd corners of the Paris Apollinaire loved, sets the tone. Yet in another way the straining always remains, and is perhaps a function of the poet's ambiguous attitude towards originality: on the one hand he is happy to adopt and adapt the time-honoured themes of myth and folklore while on the other he is at visible pains to make his mark. As in the poems, he proves himself most at ease and most successful in an albeit limited way when he allows his sense of tradition to absorb his self-consciousness.

I propose in this chapter to look first at *L'Enchanteur pourrissant*, 'ce testament de [sa] première esthétique', then at aspects of the short stories collected in *L'Hérésiarque et Cie*, *Le Poète assassiné* and *Contes retrouvés*. To close, I shall consider the only one of Apollinaire's plays which seems to warrant attention in the context of the present monograph: *Les Mamelles de Tirésias*.

L'Enchanteur pourrissant first appeared in serial form in *Le Festin d'Esope* in 1904 and in a limited de luxe edition illustrated by André Derain in 1909, but probably dates back to 1898 in conception and partial composition. 'Onirocritique' was added as a tailpiece for the book version. Based on the thirteenth-century prose *Merlin*, an embroidered development of the Arthurian wizard with certain direct or symbolic links with Apollinaire—illegitimate birth, magical powers, captivation (metaphorical or literal) by a woman—the tale is a loosely-knit sequence of visits paid to the magician's tomb. Buried there by a woman's treachery, he is both dead and alive, being immortal. The effect of the visitations is episodic and chaotic, but the central message of the tortuous rigmarole is clear: man and woman are doomed to a separation which no love can bridge. The closing dialogue between Merlin and the Lady of the Lake underlines the possessive urge on either side, an urge which turns equality into rivalry and love into a kind of death. 'L'homme est au centre de notre éloignement; nous l'entourons comme un cercle. ... Au lieu de cette bonne vie au centre de notre éloignement, il préfère chercher à nous saisir afin que l'on s'entr'aime' (*O.C.*, i, 94). The circle is indeed a vicious one. Each sees the other as 'décevant et déloyal'. The array of witnesses that Apollinaire brings trooping on—animals, druids, Morgan Le Fay, sphinxes, three fake Wise Men, Medea, Helen, heavenly choirs, the archangel Michael, monsters, Empedocles and some of the characters mentioned in 'Zone' such as 'Enoch Elie Apollonius de Tyane' and Simon Magus ('ai-je beaucoup de noms compris?')—serve mostly to emphasise the inevitability of the pessimistic conclusion. But they, and many more I have not listed, also create the chaos which corresponds to the writer's magical powers of evocation from his eclectic reading. The principle of selection yields here to the principle of unrestrained syncretism validated by the choice of so universal a theme that creative selectivity is made almost irrelevant. It leads of course to a lack of focus but also shows an imagination brimming over with ideas, even if these are usually borrowed.

'Onirocritique' takes up the major theme—'j'avais la conscience des éternités différentes de l'homme et de la femme' (*O.C.*, i, 98, 99, 100)—in a condensed dream sequence not without its echoes of traditional legend but not overtly parading this in the manner of the body of the work. Surrealists and psychoanalysts find much to interest them and exegetes of 'La Chanson du mal-aimé' note the name Sainte-Fabeau related here to the tongues of chestnut-coloured snakes and in 'Les Sept Epées' to the fifth sword, 'un cyprès sur un tombeau', 'un flambeau'. All these images merge life and death, and all may be interpreted as phallic. All of them too are set in an unreal context with elements of fairy-tale and little evident relationship to material reality. Magic, dreaming, wishful thinking, psychosis? Eeny, meeny, miney, mo ...

Isaac Laquedem (the Wandering Jew) and Simon Magus reappear in stories collected in *L'Hérésiarque et Cie*, 'Le Passant de Prague' and 'Simon Mage' respectively. The three kings figure indirectly in 'La Rose de Hildesheim ou les trésors des Rois Mages' and direct echoes of *L'Enchanteur pourrissant* might still be heard in a story in *Le Poète assassiné*, 'Arthur roi passé roi futur'. Such continuity of reference and preoccupation, while perfectly acceptable and understandable in itself, suggests that some failure in imaginative renewal may have contributed more importantly than any physical injury to the relative dullness and unoriginality in Apollinaire's writing, thinking and, according to his friends, personality after 1916.

Rather than attempt to survey the fifty or so short stories collected in the *Œuvres complètes*, I propose to illustrate three major elements in them, namely Apollinaire's use of myth and legend, his unashamed eroticism, and his interest in language. His frequent recourse to traditional mythology, legend and folklore as the narrative basis for his tales is not necessarily the mark of a lack of imagination. Rather does it suggest that Apollinaire wished to reserve his imaginative effort for other aspects of his writing. Yet it does indicate his familiarity with and respect for traditional narrative patterns, and indeed the structures of his short stories rarely depart from those analysed in folk-tales by Vladimir Propp.[1] Repentance (in 'Le Juif latin') and virtue ('L'Infaillibilité') are rewarded; lovers are reunited ('Le Cigare romanesque') or spited ('La Rose de Hildesheim'); poets die ('La Serviette des poètes') and priests procure to maintain a tradition ('L'Otmika') or beget a hermaphrodite monster ('D'un monstre à Lyon ou l'envie'); paradoxes (of the criminal's 'sanctity' in 'Le Juif latin', of Orfei's gluttony and mortification in 'L'Hérésiarque') and coincidences (e.g. in 'Histoire d'une famille vertueuse, d'une hotte et d'un calcul') abound; gruesome interest is shown in the impaling of a lovely boy ('Le Giton'), in gratuitous violence ('Un beau film') and in the eating of human flesh ('Cox-City'); the Holy Trinity appears (in 'L'Hérésiarque') as does the eternal triangle (e.g. in 'La Disparition d'Honoré Subrac' and 'Le Matelot d'Amsterdam');

and the supernatural which so appealed to nineteenth-century writers frequently figures. These examples taken from *L'Hérésiarque et Cie* could not only be multiplied by reference to later stories but their development and pursuit traced in them.

One less traditional and rather revealing subject which occurs in the later collections is pseudo-science or scientific experiment that is monstrously abused. Just as the evangelising obsession of the botanist Horace Tograth in 'Le Poète assassiné' leads to totalitarian intolerance and Croniamental's death, so in 'Train de guerre' people are wired up to produce energy, in 'Le Toucher à distance' a discovery is abused and brings about a false second coming, in 'L'Orangeade' a doctor kills his patient to discover how he has managed to cure him, and in 'Chirurgie esthétique' the monsters of mythology are brought to life by the liberal addition of eyes, noses and teeth presented in a dead-pan manner that distances the monstrosity only by setting the tale in Alaska. Such reference to science, along with tales where men become invisible (e.g. 'La Disparition d'Honoré Subrac') and others where a 'time machine' is brought into play (e.g. 'Traitement thyroïdien'), seem to reflect familiarity with the work of H. G. Wells whom Apollinaire asks in November 1915 to 'indiquer un moyen pratique de réaliser la machine à explorer le temps et l'homme invisible, procédés qui rendraient les plus grands services dans cette guerre' (*O.C.*, ii, 467). It is a war in which, as we remember from 'Il y a' in *Calligrammes*, 'l'art de l'invisibilité' plays an important role. Just so there is much artlessness concealing art in Apollinaire's stories, and the art might go unnoticed were it not that in a relatively undemanding and usually entertaining way it proves a good companion to our leisure. If we are looking for variety of tone and topic—the pathetic interspersed with the outrageous, the erotic with the exotic, the quest with the discovery—in a language always alert and sometimes very self-aware, we are likely to find Apollinaire's prose pleasant reading.

If, in addition, we are titillated by licentious tales where men are men and women are horizontal, Apollinaire will also prove stimulating if again unoriginal. Yet he clearly enjoys his literary eroticism: it is not simply for him a means of earning necessary extra cash. In the short stories there is already some variety of intercourse and the occasional homosexual ('La Rencontre au cercle mixte') or pederastic ('Le Giton') implication. There is the same breezy gusto about sexuality as one finds in such medieval or Renaissance tales as *Les Cent Nouvelles Nouvelles* or those of Chaucer, Boccaccio or Rabelais. Aretino and Sade, for whose works Apollinaire wrote introductions of no mean interest, are part of the tradition continued here. The lusty relish should not be taken, in a cold climate, to be the over-compensation for puritanical repressions: it is the frank enjoyment of an Italo-Slav. Yet, as Apollinaire reminds us, 'Il serait injuste d'attribuer à un auteur tout ce qu'il lui plaît de prêter aux personnages de son imagination' (*O.C.*, ii, 79). At least we may say that all the written evidence suggests a sustained interest in sexual matters and in a wide range of sexual practices. Repetition would be even more tedious were it not often accompanied by humour, sexual intercourse generally being treated not as an end in itself (as is the tendency in pornography) but as a narrative means. In this respect, the uncollected *Les Onze Mille Verges* is exemplary, being a sheer escapist romp. *La Fin de Babylone* (of disputed attribution and again not collected in the *Œuvres complètes*) relies less on fantasy and humour and more on the exotic lure of an escapist 'mystic orient'. *Les Trois Don Juan* is a re-telling of the well-known tale as handled by Tirso de Molina, Mérimée and Byron. A dash of Molière adds flavour, but the mixture smacks essentially of Apollinaire's particular sense of humour and eroticism. No apology is made for borrowing from *El Burlador de Sevilla*, *Les Ames du purgatoire*, *Don Juan* and *Dom Juan*, and clearly Apollinaire considered none necessary. Such archetypes belonged to the public domain and could be re-used and re-fashioned at will.

What gives such work its interest is the particular tone and style created by the language, and it is here that we detect the poet behind the *prosateur*. Not only is there precision and elegance, there is also a conscious display of language. This shows in the rare words Apollinaire is so fond of, in verbal play, and in the use of dialects for particular effect. Several rare words featuring in the poems also occur in the prose. 'Egypans' and 'pyraustes' (*O.C.*, i, 68) will be recalled from 'La Chanson du mal-aimé'; in 'Que vlo-ve?' one finds both 'la maclotte' (cf.

'Marie') and 'les pouhons' (cf. 'La Petite Auto'). Apollinaire is clearly no more afraid than Jules Verne of stepping outside the average reader's lexical range to heighten the effect of strangeness and wonder while still hoping to win popularity. Yet there is often a gratuitous element in Apollinaire's choice, even if this is governed by euphonic considerations, and opacity increases the more he departs from a recognisably French word: consider the sequence 'feuilloler', 'foleur', 'înel', 'pihis'. Apollinaire's delight in language is anecdotal rather than profound: he uses his disparate knowledge to surprise and impress. Yet that delight is real enough. In 'Simon Mage' palindromes are accorded magical significance beyond the simple play of letters. In 'La Lèpre' the coincidence of the words for 'leprosy' and 'hare' in Italian provides the basis of the tale. Puns abound, 'le calembour créateur' of Apollinaire's poetry, suggesting once again a poet's interest in the texture of words as well as their primary sense. Certainly this is also the case, though in an essentially serious way, where Apollinaire's ear for particular modes of speech, and notably of dialects, gives rise to writing of enormous brio as he transcribes such speech to give a special flavour as well as local colour to his work. Here, his international background and sojourns in various parts of Europe play an important part. But most of all he reveals an extraordinary capacity to listen and transcribe carefully. Like a thieving jackdaw he seizes jewels and gewgaws alike, but the power of such tales as 'Que vlo-ve?' and 'Les Pèlerins piémontais' is undoubtedly heightened by Apollinaire's appropriation of language to his subject.

A more ambitious tale like 'Le Poète assassiné' mixes these ingredients as before, but its extra length taxes Apollinaire's narrative inventiveness. It becomes episodic and shows more clearly its dependence on earlier models. Rabelais is much in evidence, not only in the biographical presentation of the Gargantuan hero, Croniamental, but also in many a point of detail. His humorous techniques and subjects of predilection are apparent in the following extracts:

> Tous ces peuples ont plus ou moins modifié le nom sonore de Croniamental. Les Arabes, les Turcs et autres peuples qui lisent de

droite à gauche n'ont pas manqué de le prononcer Latnamaïnorc, mais les Turcs l'appellent bizarrement Pata, ce qui signifie oie ou organe viril, à volonté. Les Russes le surnomment Viperdoc, c'est-à-dire né d'un pet ... (*O.C.*, i, 231)

'Que dis-je, ô mon ventre? tu es cruel, tu sépares les enfants de leurs pères. Non! je ne t'aime plus. Tu n'es qu'un sac plein, à cette heure, ô mon ventre souriant du nombril, ô mon ventre élastique, barbu, lisse, bombé, douloureux, rond, soyeux, qui anoblis...' (ibid., 233)

La foule des buveurs altérés poussa un cri de satisfaction. Les quatre garçons venaient d'apparaître à la porte de la brasserie. Ils portaient dignement une sorte de baldaquin sous lequel l'Oberkellner marchait raide et fier comme un roi nègre détrôné. Ils précédaient de nouveaux tonneaux de bière qui furent mis en perce au son de la cloche, et tandis qu'éclataient les rires, les cris et les chansons sur cette butte grouillante, dure et agitée comme la pomme d'Adam de Gambrinus même, quand burlesquement vêtu en moine, le radis blanc d'une main, il vide de l'autre la cruche qui lui réjouit le gosier. (ibid., 241)

Le maître de Croniamental lui fit consacrer la majeure partie de son temps aux sciences, il le tenait au courant des inventions nouvelles. Il lui enseignait aussi le latin et le grec... Il lui donna surtout le goût des anciens auteurs français. Parmi les poètes français, il estimait avant tout Villon, Ronsard et sa pléiade, Racine et La Fontaine. Il lui fit encore lire les traductions de Cervantès et de Goethe. Sur son conseil, Croniamental lut des romans de chevalerie dont plusieurs auraient pu faire partie de la bibliothèque de Don Quichotte. Ils développèrent en Croniamental un goût insurmontable pour les aventures et les amours périlleuses; il s'appliquait à l'escrime, à l'équitation; dès l'âge de quinze ans il déclarait à quiconque venait les visiter qu'il était bien décidé à devenir un chevalier fameux sans maître, et déjà il rêvait d'une maîtresse. (ibid., 250-1)

Croniamental se tut un instant puis il ajouta:
—Je n'écrirai plus qu'une poésie libre de toute entrave, serait-ce celle du langage.
Ecoute, mon vieux!

MAHÉVIDANOMI RENANOCALIPNODITOC
EXTARTINAP + v.s.
A.Z.
TÉL.: 33-122   Pan : Pan
OeaoiiiioKTin
iiiiiiiiiiii

(ibid., 257)

Examples could be multiplied *ad libitum*. Yet Croniamental is also a poet, and there are both many thinly-disguised autobiographical episodes and references and many an occasion when Apollinaire presents or parodies various views of poetry. Indeed the unequal battle between the philistines and the poet provides the ending to the story. But many details are worth noting in this respect. The line given in the last quotation above and which is there exemplified, 'Je n'écrirai plus qu'une poésie libre de toute entrave, serait-ce celle du langage', may seem extreme and nonsensical. Yet if one thinks of 'La Victoire' (see above, pp. 60–1), it clearly represents a real temptation to Apollinaire. In the same vein may be considered one of his briefest *boutades*:

J'ai fait hier mon dernier poème en vers réguliers:

> Luth
> Zut!

(O.C., i, 256)

A concise form indeed of iconoclastic wit, resuming in one word a whole Orphic tradition and in another its overthrow! It is as if Rimbaud's 'Album zutique' were pitted against Musset's 'Poète, prends ton luth ...' in 'La Nuit de mai', and the battle won with a single stroke of the pen. Such deftness and lightness of touch may also be seen in the bantering multilingualism of some suggested rhymes: should 'Sam Mac Vea' rhyme with 's'affligea' or 'écrivit', 'Rosendael' with 'réel' (*O.C.*, i, 275–6)? The point is neatly thrust home when two entirely French words, 'différent' and 'connurent' are described as 'rimant richement': 'ils contiennent une dissonance qui fait contraster délicatement le son plein des rimes masculines avec la morbidesse des féminines' (*O.C.*, i, 276). It is a nicely-judged spoof allowing Apollinaire's interest in the craft of poetry to join his delight in language to humorous effect.

It is scarcely surprising that Apollinaire should have proved good company to his friends nor indeed that they should have served as models for some of his characters. In Tristouse Balerinette and l'oiseau du Bénin of 'Le Poète assassiné' we have evocations of Marie Laurencin and Pablo Picasso. Picasso figures too as Pablo Canouris with Moïse Deléchelle (Max Jacob—'de l'échelle'!) in *La Femme assise*, an even less thinly-veiled autobiographical narrative recalling Apollinaire's *belle époque*. While it is of some interest to have Apollinaire's reminiscences of Picasso and others (see e.g. *O.C.*, i, 377, 422–3, 439–40), it may be taken that the tale in itself is of only passing concern: as prose it is remembered mostly by the cultural historian of the period.

Only specialists too seem to resuscitate *Les Mamelles de Tirésias* and I am bound to say I think it a shame, for it has a boisterous roistering quality about it which makes it no less a romp in performance than its illustrious predecessor, Jarry's *Ubu roi*. Both plays are episodic, both borrow from medieval sources and both offer the slapstick fun of the circus ring and belly-laughs galore. Many an Artaud theory is there anticipated, and likewise many a *nouveau théâtre* play. The story is slight and vulgar, the repopulation of France after the depredations of war. If it has its serious side, Apollinaire reserves it for the prefatory remarks; in the play itself, the proliferation (in the Ionesco manner) of balloons symbolic of breasts bears the message of the farce to an appropriately festive conclusion. The interest of the play, it must be confessed, lies not so much in the body of it, written in 1903, as in the prologue, added in late 1916. In it, the 'directeur de la troupe' presents certain ideas about the theatre which, while borrowing something from the recent production of *Parade* (which had its première on 8 May 1917 and for which Apollinaire wrote a programme note using the word 'surréalisme' for the first time: see *O.C.*, iv, 444 and below, p. 103), suggests the main lines of a theatrical programme which have been fruitfully pursued and as yet by no means exhausted. In *Parade*, the result of collaboration between Picasso, Erik Satie, Leonid Massine and Jean Cocteau, Apollinaire saw an expression of his own theories about 'l'Esprit nouveau' (see below, pp. 90–3) and looked forward to 'l'allégresse universelle'. In his prologue to *Les Mamelles de Tirésias*, he clearly hopes to persuade his readers and spectators that the following pantomime partakes of the new spirit, and while in the event we are hardly persuaded, some passages from the prologue will show not only how proficient an exponent of the latest ideas Apollinaire can be but also how seminal may prove even apparently outrageous experiments and attitudes:

> On tente ici d'infuser un esprit nouveau au théâtre
>
> ...
>
> La pièce a été faite pour une scène ancienne

Car on ne nous aurait pas construit de théâtre nouveau
Un théâtre rond à deux scènes
Une au centre l'autre formant comme un anneau
Autour des spectateurs et qui permettra
Le grand déploiement de notre art moderne
Mariant souvent sans lien apparent comme dans la vie
Les sons les gestes les couleurs les cris les bruits
La musique la danse l'acrobatie la poésie la peinture
Les chœurs les actions et les décors multiples

Vous trouverez ici des actions
Qui s'ajoutent au drame principal et l'ornent
Les changements de ton du pathétique au burlesque
Et l'usage raisonnable des invraisemblances
Ainsi que des acteurs collectifs ou non
Qui ne sont pas forcément extraits de l'humanité
Mais de l'univers entier
Car le théâtre ne doit pas être un art en trompe-l'œil

Il est juste que le dramaturge se serve
De tous les mirages qu'il a à sa disposition
Comme faisait Morgane sur le Mont-Gibel
Il est juste qu'il fasse parler les foules les objets inanimés
S'il lui plaît
Et qu'il ne tienne pas plus compte du temps
Que de l'espace

Son univers est sa pièce
A l'intérieur de laquelle il est le dieu créateur
Qui dispose à son gré
Les sons les gestes les démarches les masses les couleurs
Non pas dans le seul but
De photographier ce que l'on appelle une tranche de vie
Mais pour faire surgir la vie même dans toute sa vérité
Car la pièce doit être un univers complet

(*O.C.*, iii, 619–20)

The stage Apollinaire imagines, a theatre in the round with a central stage and a second circular one around the outside of the audience, may not have been constructed but in effect has been used in many a production still considered experimental. The collaboration of different arts with a view to 'total theatre' is equally familiar now, owing more to the circus and music hall than to the traditional proscenium-arch theatre, and developed in their different areas by such innovators, theorists and practitioners as Claudel, Artaud and Jean-Louis Barrault. Part of Apollinaire's programme is a specific reversal of the time-honoured neo-classical norms of the French theatre: he calls for variety of tone (such as many a neo-classical French critic condemned in Shakespeare), 'l'usage raisonnable des invraisemblances', and rejection of the unities of time, place and action. Such an overthrow of established conventions is a healthy and necessary step which we should not condemn just because it might lead to a different but equally limiting orthodoxy. For it in turn would be overthrown either by the swing of the pendulum of fashion or by the creative iconoclasm of a new Apollinaire.

VI

CRITICAL WRITINGS

The prologue to *Les Mamelles de Tirésias* is somewhat exceptional in Apollinaire's work in that for once the presentation of a theory is more interesting than the practice it reflected. Both in his writings on literature and in his art criticism his exploratory spirit was at variance with the prosaic need for consistency. His susceptibility to influence and appealing but often injudicious capacity for excitement at novelty militated against sureness in his aesthetic stance. His limitations are also his virtues. Some of the blame may be attributed to the fact that as a critic he was a journalist, with all the pressures that implies. But some of the fault is temperamental: variety is simply one side of the coin of which the other is instability.

Apollinaire's literary judgements are assembled under four headings in the *Œuvres complètes*: 'Les Diables amoureux', 'Anecdotiques', 'Chroniques. Critiques' and 'Critique littéraire', occupying the bulk of volume ii and the end of volume iii. 'Anecdotiques' and 'Chroniques. Critiques' are also much concerned with other arts, notably painting and music, and a great deal of gossip. 'Les Diables amoureux' collects the prefaces which Apollinaire wrote for two series published by the Briffaut brothers (who also printed *Le Poète assassiné*, *Les Trois Don Juan* and *La Fin de Babylone*): 'Les Maîtres de l'amour' and 'Le Coffret du bibliophile'. While the works selected for republication were certainly for adults only, they were not actually clandestine in the Paris of the time (though John Cleland's *Fanny Hill*, which Apollinaire had included, still provoked court proceedings in the Britain of the 1960s). Apollinaire certainly played a part in bringing Sade to the attention of a wider public, arguing of *Les 120 jours de Sodome*, for example, that 'le marquis de Sade y condensait toutes ses théories nouvelles et y créait ainsi, cent ans avant le docteur Krafft-Ebing, la psychopathie sexuelle' (*O.C.*, ii, 237). His moral posture is the familiar (and spurious) one that as Sade was true to his nature he cannot be condemned.

Of greater interest to my present reader are likely to be

Apollinaire's reactions to other French poets. As soon as the copyright expired on Baudelaire's work, in 1917, Apollinaire presented *Les Fleurs du mal* to the public suggesting strong affiliations with Cholderlos de Laclos and Edgar Allan Poe; and 'à ceux qu'étonnerait sa naissance infime de la boue révolutionnaire et de la vérole américaine, il faudrait répondre par ce qu'enseigne la Bible touchant l'origine de l'homme issu du limon de la terre' (ibid., 287). The idiosyncratic nature of Apollinaire's views may be judged from his reproach that 'Baudelaire n'a pas pénétré cet esprit nouveau dont il était lui-même pénétré' (ibid.) for Apollinaire had very definite ideas about what he understood by 'l'esprit nouveau' and seems unaware of the fact that while he may find evidence of it in Baudelaire, Baudelaire was ill placed to penetrate Apollinaire's thinking on the subject. The criticism is jerky and unbalanced: consider the one-sidedness of the following statement: 'Baudelaire regardait la vie avec une passion dégoûtée qui visait à transformer arbres, fleurs, femmes, l'univers tout entier et l'art même, en quelque chose de pernicieux' (*O.C.*, ii, 288). The poet who only six years before had taken some pride in not knowing Baudelaire 'dans le texte' (*O.C.*, iv, 752) was out of sympathy with a poet whom he nonetheless felt bound to admire, and sympathy was the touchstone of Apollinaire's critical judgement. A clear contrast may be seen in the case of another nineteenth-century poet: in the same letter of 1911, Apollinaire writes: 'Je connais de Gérard de Nerval quelques sonnets intitulés *Les Chimères*', yet on 16 July of that year on the basis of that knowledge and a great deal of gossip and anecdote he declares: 'Esprit charmant! Je l'eusse aimé comme un frère' (*O.C.*, ii, 324). 'Gérard de Nerval rêvait d'une poésie obscure et harmonieuse ... en France le mystère, dans la poésie, n'est peut-être pas moins légitime que la clarté' (ibid., 325).

Twice he confronts Claudel and Rimbaud in letters to Madeleine Pagès dating from 1915:

Vous m'avez parlé de Claudel dernièrement. Cet écrivain de talent est l'aboutissant du symbolisme. Il représente de façon absconse et réactionnaire la menue monnaie d'Arthur Rimbaud. Celui-ci était un Louis d'or dont celui-là est le billon. Claudel est un homme de talent qui n'a fait que des choses faciles dans le sublime. A une époque où il n'y a plus de

règles littéraires, il est facile d'en imposer. Il n'a pas eu le courage de se
dépasser et surtout de dépasser la littérature d'images qui est aujour-
d'hui facile. On s'est habitué aux images. Il n'en est plus d'inacceptables
et tout peut être symbolisé par tout. Une littérature faite d'images
enchaînées comme grains de chapelet est bonne tout au plus p[ou]r les
snobs férus de mysticité. (*O.C.*, iv, 482-3)

Et il est de fait que malgré ce que j'avais à dire contre l'esprit
froidement lyrique, le Thomisme volontairement rétrograde d'un
Claudel, celui-ci domine tout l'art connu des grands journaux et
cependant ce n'est encore là que le billon de l'or fin que fut Rimbaud.
Voilà. (ibid., 498)

The final 'Voilà' suggests not only the absolutism of Apollinaire's
judgement but also, let us hope, the fact that he was aware of its
too facile finality, geared to a correspondent he wanted to
impress. He is no less absolute, however, about a performance of
Claudel's *L'Echange*, writing of its 'poésie factice' despite 'de
vigoureuses et saines qualités'. Any compliment is thoroughly
backhanded: 'le théâtre est tombé si bas, que celui de Claudel
reste encore la seule chose qui vaille, aujourd'hui, la peine qu'on
s'en occupe' (*O.C.*, iii, 885). Of his view of Laforgue 'dont j'ai
peu lu et qui m'est fortement antipathique' (ibid., 754), a view
where sheer ignorance becomes a matter of pride, the least said
the better.

Such random thrusts characterise Apollinaire's criticism. He
was, it must always be remembered, a journalist in the matter as
well as a poet, and the balance between insights and dross is
inevitably uneven. 'N'oubliez pas que je vis entièrement de ma
plume' (*O.C.*, iv, 760). The fact doubtless explains in part some
of the inconsistencies one finds, one of which it is instructive to
trace by way of example since the matter bears closely on one of
the more novel aspects of his writing: I refer to the Italian
futurist movement. While the following sequence does not of
course pretend to be exhaustive, it does show how Apollinaire
can, via the people he meets, warm to a subject and be thoroughly absorbed by it, particularly when he feels he can claim to
have influenced it, before moving on to a new preoccupation and
seeing the previous one in a clearer perspective.

Although *Le Figaro* published Marinetti's Futurist Manifesto
on 20 February 1909, Apollinaire seems not to have begun to

show any special interest in the movement until meeting some of its early adherents. In the *Mercure de France* of 16 November 1911, he records his impressions of a meeting with Boccioni and Severini, and from a mere description of two of the former's works declares: 'Cette peinture, qui ainsi expliquée paraît avant tout sentimentale et un peu puérile, les futuristes la défendent, le cas échéant, à coups de bâton' (*O.C.*, ii, 335). In a letter to the Italian artist and critic Ardengo Soffici of 26 January 1912, Apollinaire feels free to generalise on the basis of his ignorance:

> En littérature, ... la médiocrité se tient toujours au premier rang car les médiocres ne sont pas paresseux, ils travaillent sans peine. Et soyez assuré que vos futuristes feront leur chemin en Italie. A vrai dire je ne connais pas encore leur peinture mais je me doute de ce qu'elle doit être. Si ces gens avaient un succès de presse ici je n'en serais point étonné. La publicité aurait ainsi porté ses fruits. Et vous savez que la publicité est beaucoup aujourd'hui. (*O.C.*, iv, 758–9)

Within a fortnight, on 7 and 9 February 1912, Apollinaire is himself publicising the Futurists' Paris exhibition in *L'Intransigeant* and *Le Petit Bleu* respectively and singling out for praise the two painters he had met: 'Severini est avec Boccioni le peintre qui me paraît avoir le plus à dire parmi les futuristes' (*O.C.*, iv, 231). But referring to the 'Manifeste des peintres futuristes' of 11 April 1910, Apollinaire declares it 'plein de pauvretés d'idées antiplastiques' and continues:

> L'originalité de l'école futuriste de peinture, c'est qu'elle veut reproduire le mouvement. C'est là une recherche parfaitement légitime, mais il y a belle lurette que les peintres français ont résolu ce problème dans la mesure où il peut être résolu.
>
> En réalité, les peintres futuristes ont eu jusqu'ici plus d'idées philosophiques et littéraires que d'idées plastiques. (*O.C.*, iv, 230)

Condescension mixes with chauvinism, and Apollinaire seems to rely heavily on Picasso's reaction to the painting:

> Le peintre Picasso regarde une toile d'un peintre futuriste. Elle est fort embrouillée, des objets disparates s'y mêlent: une bouteille, un faux col, une tête d'homme jovial, etc., ce désordre est intitulé *Le Rire*.
> —C'est plutôt *Le Pêle-Mêle*, dit en souriant Picasso. (*O.C.*, ii, 348)

Apollinaire's confession to being intrigued by the literary ideas of the futurists reminds us that the ensuing months of 1912 saw the composition of the last poems to be included in *Alcools*, including 'Zone' which undoubtedly owes to them some of its daring. And 'reproduire le mouvement' also recalls a number of poems, particularly from the opening section of *Calligrammes*. It may even be recognised that literary and philosophical ideas gleaned from the futurists sustained Apollinaire through the horrors of war (see below, pp. 116)

For the next important appearance of futurist notions in his writings suggests that he has adopted totally the puerile stance he had so loftily dismissed on first acquaintance. It is his own contribution to the series of futurist manifestos, 'L'Antitradition futuriste' dated 29 June 1913, in which he distributes accolades or otherwise to various writers, painters, movements, and even towns and countries. Marinetti is given pride of place in two of the approving lists, being named first for a 'rose' and having his 'Mots en liberté' head the bold-type entries under the title 'construction'. Apollinaire seems to have allowed his judgement to have been thoroughly subsumed by the Italian, and his posturing leads to rank silliness. 'Merde' is distributed to a rag-bag of more or less deserving causes: 'Critiques Pédagogues Professeurs ... Dante Shakespeare Tolstoï Goethe ... Montaigne Wagner Beethoven Edgard [*sic*] Poe Walt Whitman et Baudelaire' (for a facsimile of the original see *O.C.*, iii, following p. 876). Roses are reserved no less indiscriminately for the memorable and the eminently forgettable: 'Marinetti Picasso Boccioni Apollinaire ... Rubiner Bétuda Manzella-Frontini A. Mazza ... etc.'. A month later, writing again to Soffici, Apollinaire claims 'Onirocritique' as a precursor of futurism and spreads the gallocentric net:

... je sais que des morceaux comme l'*Onirocritique* (*Phalange* 1908) ont eu une importance quant à la voie qu'a prise le mouvement moderne et particulièrement le futurisme. Marinetti le sait et c'est pour cela que je tente cette synthèse de tous les efforts artistiques nouveaux, mais vous Italiens, ne soyez pas injustes envers les Français car ils ont inventé presque tous [*sic*] le modernisme intellectuel de même qu'ils se trouvent au premier rang en ce qui concerne les inventions scientifiques de notre âge. (*O.C.*, iv, 760)

A claim to originality overrides more balanced and cogent considerations and allows Apollinaire to identify his efforts with those of the futurists. Personalities have much to do with it, for Apollinaire now knows the leader of the movement: 'Marinetti est un homme charmant et un vrai poète, plus je le vois, plus je l'estime' (ibid., 761). And on 10 October 1913, while condemning in Boccioni the same chauvinism of which he himself is guilty, he states roundly: 'Vous savez combien je suis sympathique au mouvement futuriste' (ibid.).

Disenchantment seems to stem from pique both personal and patriotic: the futurists are unwilling to recognise French sources (French like Picasso, French like Apollinaire!) and in *Les Soirées de Paris* of 15 February 1914 we read:

> Les mots en liberté, eux, peuvent bouleverser les syntaxes, les rendre plus souples, plus brèves; ils peuvent généraliser l'emploi du style télégraphique. Mais quant à l'esprit même, au sens intime et moderne et sublime de la poésie, rien de changé, sinon qu'il y a plus de rapidité, plus de facettes descriptibles et décrites, mais tout de même éloignement de la nature, car les gens ne parlent point au moyen de mots en liberté. Les mots en liberté de Marinetti amènent un renouvellement de la description et à ce titre ils ont de l'importance, ils amènent également un retour offensif de la description et ainsi ils sont didactiques et antilyriques. (*O.C.*, iii, 884)

By October 1916, Apollinaire writes more detachedly when drawing the attention of *Mercure de France* readers to Marinetti's latest tract outlining 'la nouvelle religion de la vélocité' (*O.C.*, ii, 480). And in his recognition of the virtues of exaggeration we see perhaps an apologia for his own positions:

> L'exagération est aussi sans doute une vélocité. Et il y a quelque prétention choquante à vouloir tout de go fonder une religion dont le besoin ne se fait pas sentir. Mais il n'en reste pas moins que les moyens de locomotion, le mouvement pour tout dire, ont modifié notre façon de sentir, lui ont donné un prétexte excellent pour se renouveler, et il y a quelque chose de juste et de touchant dans ce désir de nouveau qui, né en France, s'exprime si violemment en Italie. Il y a là sinon une religion, du moins comme une morale de la nouveauté qui a quelque sens, dès qu'on le débarrasse des concetti marinettiens. Et puis comment ne pas regarder avec sympathie un homme qui ne cesse d'insuffler le courage au cœur de ses compatriotes? (*O.C.*, ii, 482)

But patriotism in time of war is not enough. Apollinaire recognises 'l'autorité un peu étroite du pape Marinetti' (ibid., 484), acknowledging now (as he had not done in writing 'L'Antitradition futuriste') the danger of what Jean Paulhan was to call 'la terreur dans les lettres'. Such literary terrorism, a forerunner of surrealist and structuralist coteries, affected Apollinaire whose *disponibilité* far exceeded his potential as a *chef d'école*. Despite his claim: 'Je suis cependant d'une époque où mes camarades et moi n'aimions point nous ranger ni à la suite de quelqu'un ni en groupes arrivistes' (*O.C.*, iii, 888), Apollinaire shows that in respect of futurism he did precisely that for a time in the spirit if not in the letter.

The tale traced here, typical enough of Apollinaire's critical postures, is instructive. For it shows his susceptibility to personalities rather than to ideas or the works of art themselves and the consequent instability of his stance. It also shows how completely and sometimes unquestioningly he used everyone else's grist in his own mill: legitimate enough in a poet, unpardonable in a critic. One could trace his reversal of attitude towards the painters Rouault, Delaunay or Rousseau ('le Douanier') to similar causes of prejudiced ignorance melting on acquaintance with the man behind the brush into prejudiced praise. It means that one can select sporadic insights for quotation and give a false impression of judicious perspicacity: it is easy to forget chaff when someone else has done the winnowing. Limitations of space and patience make it imperative to *avoid* keeping Apollinaire's own balance between the jejune and the perceptive, the journalistic and the poetic. But to be fair it seems appropriate to consider one of his more extended and celebrated excursions into literary theorising not simply for the way in which it summarises much of his thinking about poetry in the last years of his life but also for its intrinsic interest as a manifesto of the time: 'L'Esprit nouveau et les poètes', given first as a lecture on 26 November 1917 and published in the *Mercure de France* a year later:

L'esprit nouveau qui s'annonce prétend avant tout hériter des classiques un solide bon sens, un esprit critique assuré, des vues d'ensemble sur l'univers et dans l'âme humaine, et le sens du devoir qui dépouille les sentiments et en limite ou plutôt en contient les manifestations.

Il prétend encore hériter des romantiques une curiosité qui le pousse à explorer tous les domaines propres à fournir une matière littéraire qui permette d'exalter la vie sous quelque forme qu'elle se présente.

Explorer la vérité, la chercher, aussi bien dans le domaine ethnique, par exemple, que dans celui de l'imagination, voilà les principaux caractères de cet esprit nouveau. (*O.C.*, iii, 900)

Nothing particularly novel so far. But the poet, for example, has a new-found freedom and it is his duty to take advantage of it:

Le vers libre donna un libre essor au lyrisme ...
Les recherches dans la forme ont repris désormais une grande importance.

...
Les artifices typographiques poussés très loin avec une grande audace ont l'avantage de faire naître un lyrisme visuel qui était presque inconnu avant notre époque. Ces artifices peuvent aller très loin encore et consommer la synthèse des arts, de la musique, de la peinture et de la littérature. (*O.C.*, iii, 901)

If by 'un lyrisme visuel' Apollinaire is clearly designating his own calligrammes, he has not yet specified whether the consummate synthesis of the arts he envisages is meant to follow Wagner's *Gesamtkunstwerk* or Mallarmé's *Grand Œuvre*. In fact it is neither, for it depends on a medium neither of them knew: the cinema.

Il eût été étrange qu'à une époque où l'art populaire par excellence, le cinéma, est un livre d'images, les poètes n'eussent pas essayé de composer des images pour les esprits méditatifs et plus raffinés qui ne se contentent point des imaginations grossières des fabricants de films. Ceux-ci se raffineront, et l'on peut prévoir le jour où le phonographe et le cinéma étant devenus les seules formes d'impression en usage, les poètes auront une liberté inconnue jusqu'à présent.
Qu'on ne s'étonne point si, avec les seuls moyens dont ils disposent encore, ils s'efforcent de se préparer à cet art nouveau (plus vaste que l'art simple des paroles) où, chefs d'un orchestre d'une étendue inouïe, ils auront à leur disposition: le monde entier, ses rumeurs et ses apparences, la pensée et le langage humain, le chant, la danse, tous les arts et tous les artifices, plus de mirages encore que ceux que pouvait faire surgir Morgane sur le mont Gibel pour composer le livre vu et entendu de l'avenir. (*O.C.*, iii, 901–2)

Michel Butor makes a fair assessment of the positive force of this vision:

Apollinaire a été un des premiers à comprendre poétiquement qu'une révolution culturelle était impliquée par l'apparition de nouveaux moyens de reproduction et de transmission, que le phonographe, le téléphone, la radio et le cinéma (sans parler de la télévision et de l'enregistrement magnétique), moyens de conserver et diffuser le langage ou l'histoire sans passer par l'intermédiaire de l'écriture, obligeait à poser sur celle-ci un regard nouveau, à interroger cet objet fondamental de notre civilisation qu'est le livre.[1]

Yet within Apollinaire's own development there has evidently been little renewal, for in *Les Soirées de Paris* of February 1914 he had expounded the same idea essentially borrowed from Marinetti:

> Avant peu, les poètes pourront, au moyen des disques, lancer à travers le monde de véritables poèmes symphoniques. ...
> A la poésie horizontale que l'on n'abandonnera point pour cela, s'ajoutera une poésie verticale, ou polyphonique, dont on peut attendre des œuvres fortes et imprévues. (*O.C.*, iii, 884)

Rejecting the disorder of Marinetti and his group, however, Apollinaire extols the French 'horreur du chaos' (*O.C.*, iii, 902) and says that 'cette synthèse des arts ... ne doit pas dégénérer en une confusion' (ibid., 903). Although its materials may be the noise of machinery and other recent inventions, it must remain lyrical; but Apollinaire is unwilling or unable to explore the paradoxical nature of such a plea, only confusing matters further by not specifying what he understands by 'expériences ... peu lyriques' and stating that lyricism is only a part of 'l'esprit nouveau' (ibid., 904).

The mainspring he finally decides upon is the element of surprise:

> ... le nouveau existe bien, sans être un progrès. Il est tout dans la surprise. L'esprit nouveau est également dans la surprise. C'est ce qu'il y a en lui de plus vivant, de plus neuf. *La surprise est le grand ressort nouveau.* C'est par la surprise, par la place importante qu'il fait à la surprise que l'esprit nouveau se distingue de tous les mouvements artistiques et littéraires qui l'ont précédé. (*O.C.*, iii, 906)

No longer bounded by language, the poet 'peut être poète dans tous les domaines' (ibid., 907), yet the poetic imagination that Apollinaire describes is as old as poetry itself: 'Le moindre fait est pour le poète le postulat, le point de départ d'une immensité inconnue où flambent les feux de joie des significations multiples' (ibid.). Here is Apollinaire's dilemma in a nutshell: he is torn between order and adventure. Moderation would be for him a synonym and an excuse for ineffectualness. And reconciliation proves impossible: he is too partisan in turn for one or the other, just as he is too partisan about France: 'il n'y a guère de poètes aujourd'hui que de langue française', 'la France, détentrice de tout le secret de la civilisation ...' (ibid., 908). Such blinkered allegiances cannot but detract from the sensible points Apollinaire makes. Even his admirer André Breton was prompted to write:

> Et qu'a su dire Apollinaire de cet esprit moderne qu'il a passé son temps à invoquer? Il n'y a qu'à lire l'article paru quelques jours avant sa mort [in fact just after] et intitulé 'L'Esprit nouveau et les poètes', pour être frappé du néant de sa méditation et de l'inutilité de tout ce bruit.[2]

He is both winning and infuriating, and each facet of his vacillating mind must be taken in conjunction with every other.

Such fragmented wholeness shows in much the same light in Apollinaire's art criticism, to which we now turn. Judgements on his capacities as an art critic reflect their many-sidedness: a staunch literary champion, J.-Cl. Chevalier, can write:

> ... au-delà du poète improvisateur, il faut voir un critique pénétrant, depuis toujours épris d'art, autodidacte certes, mais qui a su se forger lentement et vigoureusement, aux hasards heureux de rencontres avec des peintres de génie, une théorie qui n'a en rien perdu de son actualité et permet de ranger Apollinaire à côté de Baudelaire et de Diderot.[3]

Art critics tend to be less generous, emphasising the lack of training, underlining the fact that so many ideas were gleaned straight from the painters themselves, and doubting the existence of a genuine or sufficient core of theory. Pierre Cabanne: 'Ses connaissances artistiques sont nulles ou presque: de l'histoire de l'art il ne sait rien et n'a rien vu... Il réussit ce prodige d'exalter les peintres sans jamais "parler peinture".'[4] Norbert Lynton:

> People say he loved art. Perhaps he did, but the evidence is rather that he loved artists and the idea of art and the to and fro of the art scene. He had no eye, as artists knew at once, but his ear was excellent and he could quickly pick the words for new concepts and for new formulations of old ones. He and his readers were content that he should

leave his findings in the form of rhapsodies and méditations esthétiques. The result is that a lot of the wrong-headed notions that still cling to subjects like Cubism can be traced back to him. It is also likely, though, that his kind of warm and nebulous commentary made modern art more approachable for its Paris public.[5]

John Golding: 'Apollinaire, whose enthusiasm and readiness to support any new cause (often without any very deep understanding or sympathy with its aims) did much to add to the artistic confusion of the period'.[6]

Two volumes of Apollinaire's writings form the essential basis of such divergent views: *Méditations esthétiques: Les Peintres cubistes* (1913), best known by its sub-title, and the hundreds of newspaper articles collected under the title *Chroniques d'art* (*1902–1918*) and first published thus in 1960. These works open the fourth volume of the *Œuvres complètes*. Any helpful selection of material from them is likely to be flattering to Apollinaire since as a journalist he was obliged to record the work of many an insignificant painter and was sometimes drawn into fulsome praise for the trivial and jejune. We need not dwell on all the nonentities his profession or persuasions of the moment made him note. Rather shall I concentrate here on the one book of criticism Apollinaire published during his lifetime and his relations with the movement with which his name both was at the time and is still most closely associated: cubism.

It is now apparent that although cubism fairly rapidly degenerated into the purely decorative, the original movement revolutionised attitudes to painting whose main lines had remained unchanged since the Renaissance. Cézanne's proto-cubist experiments on the basis of his observation that everything in nature takes its form from the sphere, the cone and the cylinder were as radical in changing conventions as were the extraordinarily influential discoveries formulated by the fifteenth-century polymath Leon Battista Albèrti concerning the two-dimensional representation of perspective. In the west at least the cubists were the first painters to re-order man's view of the world for over four hundred years. Picasso's revolutionary painting 'Les Demoiselles d'Avignon' (1907) marks the turning-point almost within its frame, for of the angular figures it portrays, those at the right hand side show features which will become increasingly familiar. The face of the standing figure with its stylised distortions and hatching suggests a scarified negro mask, and the seated figure is simultaneously seen from a multiplicity of angles. At Apollinaire's instigation, Braque first met Picasso at his studio and saw the painting shortly after it had been completed, and their friendship and mutual influence became such that for a period their styles were scarcely distinguishable. Braque indeed is now credited with the first cubist painting as such and the word 'cube' was first applied in writing to his work in November 1908 by the critic Louis Vauxcelles, at first analytically but in later reviews disparagingly. In *Les Peintres cubistes*, Apollinaire credits Matisse however with the first use of the epithet, in derision, in the autumn of 1908.

Apollinaire had first met Picasso in 1904 and published two articles on him in 1905. The criticism is impressionistic, not analytical, and evidently owes more to friendship with the painter than to informed judgement. Apollinaire never ceased to be a loyal promoter of Picasso's work. Indeed he was both a spokesman and a champion for many gifted artists striving to establish a reputation. Using their conversation and explanations to him about their aims but also bringing his own lyrical gifts into play, Apollinaire verbalised ideas on their behalf and incidentally helped supplement his income as a free-lance journalist. By and large his efforts were not appreciated except as publicity by the painters themselves. Braque is reported as saying:

Apollinaire [was] a great poet and a man to whom I was deeply attached but, let's face it, he couldn't tell the difference between a Raphael and a Rubens. The only value of his book on Cubism is that, far from enlightening people, it succeeds in bamboozling them.[7]

Marie Laurencin, Picasso, Marcel Duchamp, the dealer Daniel-Henry Kahnweiler and others who had benefited directly from Apollinaire's efforts joined the chorus of denigration and continued it long after the perpetrator had died.

In a sympathetic and most informative introduction to a recent edition of *Les Peintres cubistes* (Paris: Hermann, 1965), L. C. Breunig and J.-Cl. Chevalier quote (p. 28) the more favourable reaction of a reviewer, Maurice Raynal:

Dans cette sorte de poème sur la peinture qu'il [Apollinaire] vient de publier, on sent tout d'abord que sa nature principalement poétique lui défendait de commenter et d'expliquer la peinture même.

En général, les vrais poètes ne comprennent rien, mais ressentent tout. Aussi, Guillaume Apollinaire, sorte de sensualiste mystique, ne *comprend* pas la peinture, mais *la perçoit, l'éprouve.*

The editors take the same stand in a persuasive way, arguing that just as in a number of the longer poems in *Alcools* there are sharp juxtapositions and contrasts, so in *Les Peintres cubistes* 'Apollinaire a inauguré ... le genre de la "poésie critique" ' (loc. cit., p. 35). That Apollinaire himself would transfer such concepts from one medium to another is evident, and there is a particularly apposite example of it in his reference on 2 April 1913 to the word 'zones': 'cette expression excellente qui s'applique aux masses colorées des lumières impaires' (*O.C.*, iv, 304). Both *Les Peintres cubistes* and 'Zone' itself seem illuminated by such an idea which prefigures the specific aesthetics of surprise formulated in 'L'Esprit nouveau et les poètes'.

Méditations esthétiques, Apollinaire's original main title for the volume, is undoubtedly more appropriate in that it allows both fragmentation and rumination whereas *Les Peintres cubistes* suggests a history or a manifesto, 'mais la seconde partie du titre, qui aurait dû être un sous-titre a été imprimé en beaucoup plus gros caractères que la première et est devenue ainsi le titre' (*O.C.*, iv, 491). The book consists largely of brief studies published in various newspapers and journals between 1905 and 1912 and collected in two sections, 'Sur la peinture' and 'Peintres nouveaux'. The first, ejaculatory and sibylline in the manner of so much of Apollinaire's critical writing, contains general considerations and singles Picasso out for particular attention. The second groups independent vignettes of nine painters, with one sculptor in an appendix, and again gives Picasso pride of place. Each section contains a major butt for criticism: the first a classification of types of cubism ('scientifique', 'physique', 'orphique' and 'instinctif') and the second the very inclusion of Marie Laurencin as a cubist painter, which she decidedly is not. The howl raised by the proposed classification tended to make more reasonable and interesting points inaudible. Some consideration of 'Sur la peinture' may help redress the balance, showing that Apollinaire, however prompted by his painter friends (and particularly by Delaunay in the late stages of preparation of the book), grasped some of the fundamentally new aspects of cubism and presented them in an exciting if inspissating way.

La flamme est le symbole de la peinture et les trois vertus plastiques flambent en rayonnant.

La flamme a la pureté qui ne souffre rien d'étranger et transforme cruellement en elle-même ce qu'elle atteint.

Elle a cette unité magique qui fait que si on la divise, chaque flammèche est semblable à la flamme unique.

Elle a enfin la vérité sublime de sa lumière que nul ne peut nier. (*O.C.*, iv, 15–16)

This passage, first published in 1908, seems closer to 'Le Brasier' or the ending of 'Les Fiançailles' than to traditional art criticism, where metaphor is never allowed to rule so unchallenged. Almost as a rebuke to himself in certain moods, Apollinaire declares: 'Nous ne nous épuiserons pas à saisir le présent trop fugace et qui ne peut être pour l'artiste que le masque de la mort: la mode' (ibid., 17). In so doing, he is doubtless trying to intimate the sense of tradition which, so strong in him, he feels too in the painters he knows. But does this justify the unhelpful and hackneyed 'Avant tout, les artistes sont des hommes qui veulent devenir inhumains' (ibid.)? More pertinent, though still with neither stylistic analysis nor direct reference to the new role of photography in ousting the need for representational painting, are the following observations:

La vraisemblance n'a plus aucune importance, car tout est sacrifié par l'artiste aux vérités, aux nécessités d'une nature supérieure qu'il suppose sans la découvrir. Le sujet ne compte plus ou s'il compte c'est à peine.

L'art moderne repousse, généralement, la plupart des moyens de plaire mis en œuvre par les grands artistes des temps passés.

Si le but de la peinture est toujours comme il fut jadis: le plaisir des yeux, on demande désormais à l'amateur d'y trouver un autre plaisir que celui que peut lui procurer aussi bien le spectacle des choses naturelles. (*O.C.*, iv, 18)

But this is followed by further obfuscation, the relationship adumbrated between literature and music apparently being taken unquestioningly from a highly questionable Symbolist aesthetic:

On s'achemine ainsi vers un art entièrement nouveau, qui sera à la peinture, telle qu'on l'avait envisagée jusqu'ici, ce que la musique est à la littérature.

Ce sera de la peinture pure, de même que la musique est de la littérature pure. (ibid.)

The notion of a non-Euclidean fourth dimension is introduced without being related to time. It is rather 'explained' as 'la manifestation des aspirations, des inquiétudes d'un grand nombre de jeunes artistes . . . attendant un art sublime' (ibid., 21). It needs the aesthetic vagueness of an Apollinaire to dare such generalisations. There is considerable naïveté and romanticism too in the notion that 'les poètes et les artistes déterminent de concert la figure de leur époque et docilement l'avenir se range à leur avis' (ibid.). Such manifest if appealing balderdash serves only to obscure the validity of other points Apollinaire makes, including an awareness of cultural relativism (in part vi of his essay) and of the intellectual qualities of cubism (in part vii): 'Ce qui différencie le cubisme de l'ancienne peinture, c'est qu'il n'est pas un art d'imitation, mais un art de conception qui tend à s'élever jusqu'à la création' (ibid., 24). Apollinaire's point of comparison is almost certainly impressionism, whose 'déroute' he welcomed in his review of the Salon des Indépendants in 1910 (*O.C.*, iv, 107) in hailing a return to 'composition' (ibid., 116). The sense of order, indeed of a new order, perceived by Apollinaire in the geometry of cubist paintings tallies with their concentration on form in contrast to the impressionists' fascination with the surface play of light. The challenge of expressing the three dimensions of reality on the two dimensions of the canvas is of course inherent in the medium, but there is no doubt that the cubists, in proposing their new solution, drew attention to the nature of the challenge afresh. And in so doing, as has already been hinted, they also involved the reciprocal challenge of simultaneity to time.

Although Apollinaire's attempt at categorising different cubist tendencies generated more heat than light, it is apparent that his aim at least reflected the scientific clarity which Picasso, Delaunay and others helped him discover in cubism. And it is noteworthy that the phrase that returns in each definition is 'ensembles nouveaux' (*O.C.*, iv, 24–5). For some years Apollinaire, prompted no doubt by his painter friends, had resisted the epithet 'cubist', not least because it had first been used in contempt (cf. 'impressionism', 'fauvism' etc.). Only in 1911 did he abandon the role of Canute and accept the inevitable. In the absence from that year's Salon des Indépendants of paintings by Picasso and Braque (who were both, particularly Picasso, reticent about prostituting their work to the public gaze), Apollinaire stated: 'Metzinger est ici le seul adepte du cubisme proprement dit', defining the movement's aim briefly in the following terms:

Cet art cinématique, en quelque sorte, a pour but de nous montrer la vérité plastique sous toutes ses faces et sans renoncer au bénéfice de la perspective. (*O.C.*, iv, 188)

In a catalogue preface of June 1911 he makes the acceptance specific: 'les peintres nouveaux qui ont manifesté ensemble au Salon des Indépendants de Paris leur idéal artistique, acceptent le nom de cubistes qu'on leur a donné' (ibid., 208). But immediately he emphasises the variety hidden by that single word, the fact that if cubism is a movement, a direction, it is not a *système*. As Breunig and Chevalier comment, 'on a ici définitivement l'impression que le poète emploie à contre-cœur un mot qui se termine en "-isme" et qu'en en élargissant tellement le sens, il veut éviter de se faire l'apologiste d'une chapelle, tout en défendant l'effort des peintres qui en font partie' (loc. cit., pp. 14–15).

'Peintres nouveaux', 'ensembles nouveaux' … 'l'esprit nouveau'. This is what really grips Apollinaire's mind. The quality of the work is scarcely recognised. Indeed in October 1911, when the greatest cubist work had already been completed, Apollinaire was still writing: 'Le cubisme est une réaction nécessaire, de laquelle, qu'on le veuille ou non, il sortira de grandes œuvres' (*O.C.*, iv, 218). If he burns his critical boats by opting for experimentation against the 'barbouilleurs présomptueux, démodés et ennuyeux des salons officiels' (ibid., 208), his discernment is inadequate to cope with the real achievements of cubism. He had the experience and missed the meaning.

It is idle to speculate as to what positive aspects of his art

criticism Apollinaire owed to his painter friends, though his
changing allegiances as he discovered new companions are docu-
mented through the very confusion they created. What is more
relevant to our present purpose is some consideration of the
influence of cubism on his poetry. The variously attributed
revelation of Negro and Oceanian sculpture has a narrative echo
at the end of 'Zone' but may also account more profoundly for
an awareness of new types of possible stylisation, a renewed
realisation that conventions are relative. But if there is any real
sense behind the often-repeated suggestion that Apollinaire
wrote 'cubist poetry', it is in the parallel though inevitably
different recognition in two media of a new spatio-temporal
challenge. The differences are sufficiently important for many
serious critics to dismiss the idea as nonsense. But the similarities
remain not only enticing but genuinely illuminating as regards
one of the most interesting aspects of Apollinaire's poetry: they
focus attention on his fragmentation of form in the search for
new forms. It is sufficient for the moment to recall the techniques
of juxtaposition at play in such poems as 'Zone' and 'La
Chanson du mal-aimé', the variety of spatial form on the page
one finds in Apollinaire's poetry generally, and the challenge of
simultaneity to duration presented not only by the calligrammes
but in more assimilated and specifically literary ways by other
poems to which attention has already been drawn.[8] To seek is
not necessarily to find. I believe the great paradox of Apollinaire
to be the general lack of coincidence between areas of achievement and areas of excitement. But for those who believe travelling is better than arriving, Apollinaire is tonic. As he himself
reminds us, 'on ne découvrira jamais la réalité une fois pour
toutes. La vérité sera toujours nouvelle. Autrement, elle n'est
qu'un système plus misérable que la nature' (*O.C.*, iv, 17), and
having writ, moves on.

When cubism itself became too much of a system for
Apollinaire's liking, he allowed his taste for novelty to attract
him towards new development in arts. Had the war and his early
death not intervened he was heading for participation in Dada
and surrealism, both of which movements he had heralded in
one way or another. As it was, they simply lie, like so many other
movements or individuals, within the magnetic field of his shadow.

VII

THE LEGACY

'Je lègue à l'avenir l'histoire de Guillaume Apollinaire'. It was indeed the story of his life that Apollinaire bequeathed rather than any concerted doctrine or consistent body of poetry. And in so writing in 'Merveille de la guerre', he seemingly authorised the literary historian or biographer to distract or even detract from his work as such. That he was a child of his times is not in question, but the times do not explain the poetry—otherwise the work of Claudel, Valéry, Apollinaire and others would be much of a muchness. Yet well before the serious critics, those who had known Apollinaire personally paved the way for an imbalance, weighing context against text, which has still not been redressed.

Apollinaire must have been an extraordinary person to know: vibrant, mysterious, amusing, outrageous, gay, fitful, enchanting, provocative, wilful, uproarious, demanding, generous, irreverent and sad. An inveterate frequenter of cafés and retailer of gossip and tall stories, his mercurial temperament—however belied by his portly figure—contributed to and often found itself the centre of a brilliant if brittle artistic society. He was happy to perpetuate legends about himself and strike a pose as archetypal poet. He played his part in a ferment of discoveries and excitement which itself has left the legend of the *belle époque*. And our image of him undoubtedly benefits from his association with the period and with some of its most memorable creative artists. Yet 'l'homme, il faut le reconnaître, est particulièrement encombrant'. And in Claude Tournadre's survey of critical attitudes introducing the helpful compilation of *Les Critiques de notre temps et Apollinaire* we read further: 'De ces mythes, Apollinaire lui-même est en partie responsable. Ses nombreux amis aussi. Ils ont pieusement servi sa mémoire, mais n'ont pas su se départir du culte de la personnalité' (p. 9).

The foreign reader, struggling with problems of linguistic comprehension and a stranger to the corridors of Parisian literary power, enjoys in consequence a singular advantage in being freer than his French counterpart from the insidious magnetism of a publicity myth or a personality cult. Even before the outbreak of war in 1914, F. S. Flint, Ezra Pound and Richard Aldington had all taken this advantage and, however tersely, published their judgements on Apollinaire's poetry.[1] Of *Alcools*, Pound wrote in 1913: 'Apollinaire has brought out a clever book'.[2] Flint's view was dictated by his French correspondent Alexandre Mercereau, the director of *Vers et prose*. In a letter to him dated 4 June 1912, Flint admits: 'Apollinaire m'a envoyé quelques poèmes. Je ne saurais trop quoi en dire', to which Mercereau replies: 'Le poète est curieux, fantaisiste, raffiné, très souple, expert en notations subtiles, aiguës, rares.'[3] Flint's only comment on Apollinaire in his long and important survey of 'Contemporary French Poetry' is a translated carbon copy of this: 'Guillaume Apollinaire [is] a curious, fantastic, keen, supple poet, expert in subtle and piercing notations'.[4] He was, however, to develop his views and make amends for his lack of originality in subsequent articles, as in his praise, *en connaissance de cause*, of *Alcools*.[5] Flint's remarkable coverage of contemporary French poets provided an important introduction for English readers, but Apollinaire is not by any means given pride of place and indeed is lost in the welter of names and thumb-nail sketches.

T. S. Eliot may be credited with certain tonal affinities with Apollinaire in his *Prufrock and other observations* (1917) and *Poems* (1920) but they stem from a common source in Laforgue and the *fantaisistes*; there was no direct influence. Eliot's 'Mr Apollinax' is clearly not Apollinaire. Indeed the Anglo-American poet seems not to have read his European contemporary until around 1920.[6] And it would appear that for other English poets of Eliot's generation, Flint's seeds fell on stony ground. Not until after the publication in 1945 of a *Choix de poésies* made by Cyril Connolly and presented by C. M. Bowra (London: Horizon) did Apollinaire gain something of a foothold on this side of the English Channel. Those who knew no French had to wait another ten years for readily accessible volumes in translation. Adulation is tempered by such circumstances. And the question remains: Was the man more interesting than his poetry?

The founder and 'pope' of surrealism, André Breton, certainly thought so, and his judgement did not simply stem from a persuasion that life is more important than literature since in the case of Reverdy he came to appreciate the writings more than the man. After initial enthusiasm for both Apollinaire and his poetry (and enthusiasm can lead to failures in differentiation of just this sort), Breton became generally disenchanted with the writings. As Anna Balakian has written, 'there is a marked difference between the fervent praise in Breton's article on Apollinaire written in 1917 while the *poète assassiné* was still living, and his more guarded references to Apollinaire in the lecture he delivered in Barcelona in 1922.'[7] But 'guarded' is scarcely the word to describe some of Breton's belittling remarks on the latter occasion: his view of 'L'Esprit nouveau et les poètes' (see above, p. 93) is not untypical. Yet as a 'flâneur des deux rives' Apollinaire led Breton to an urban poetry which is prominent for example in *Nadja* and prevalent among surrealists in general. And many an image created by Apollinaire could be considered surrealist *avant la lettre*.[8] Certainly Breton and his group developed and exploited the aesthetics of surprise and made a point of honour some of the more iconoclastic attitudes of a lineage of poets—Nerval, Rimbaud, Lautréamont—of which Apollinaire was a part-time member.

Despite considerable affinities however, it is worth noting the difference in meaning attributed to the word 'surrealism' by Apollinaire who coined it and by the surrealist movement itself. In the programme note for *Parade* Apollinaire, after indicating the novel contributions of Satie, Picasso and Massine, writes:

De cette alliance nouvelle ... il est résulté, dans *Parade*, une sorte de sur-réalisme où je vois le point de départ d'une série de manifestations de cet Esprit Nouveau qui, trouvant aujourd'hui l'occasion de se montrer, ne manquera pas de séduire l'élite et promet de modifier de fond en comble les arts et les mœurs dans l'allégresse universelle, car le bon sens veut qu'ils soient au moins à la hauteur des progrès scientifiques et industriels. (*O.C.*, iv, 444–5)

Although astonishing juxtapositions are to be a hallmark of surrealist technique, the 'alliance nouvelle' is here inadequately defined to suppose it a specific foretaste of the style, and its association with Apollinaire's 'Esprit Nouveau' makes it suspect to followers of Breton. Apollinaire tries to define the term further in his preface to *Les Mamelles de Tirésias* which he subtitles 'drame surréaliste':

> Pour caractériser mon drame je me suis servi d'un néologisme qu'on me pardonnera car cela m'arrive rarement et j'ai forgé l'adjectif sur-réaliste qui ne signifie pas du tout symbolique ... mais définit assez bien une tendance de l'art qui si elle n'est pas plus nouvelle que tout ce qui se trouve sous le soleil n'a du moins jamais servi à formuler aucun credo, aucune affirmation artistique et littéraire.
>
> ...
>
> Et pour tenter, sinon une rénovation du théâtre, du moins un effort personnel, j'ai pensé qu'il fallait revenir à la nature même, mais sans l'imiter à la manière des photographes.
>
> Quand l'homme a voulu imiter la marche, il a créé la roue qui ne ressemble pas à une jambe. Il a fait ainsi du surréalisme sans le savoir. (*O.C.*, iii, 609)[9]

'Revenir à la nature' seems to be the cry of so many utterly different schools that however often Apollinaire repeats it (either in that form or in the guise of wishing to copy real life) it can never be a guide to a specific stylistic convention. We do at least learn that he differentiates surrealist from symbolist and that the former is to reality what the wheel is to legs.

In Breton's first *Manifeste du surréalisme* (1924), we are offered the following definition:

> SURREALISME, n.m. Automatisme psychique pur par lequel on se propose d'exprimer, soit verbalement, soit par écrit, soit de toute autre manière, le fonctionnement réel de la pensée. Dictée de la pensée, en l'absence de tout contrôle exercé par la raison, en dehors de toute préoccupation esthétique ou morale.
>
> ENCYCL. *Philos.* Le surréalisme repose sur la croyance à la réalité supérieure de certaines formes d'associations négligées jusqu'à lui, à la toute-puissance du rêve, au jeu désintéressé de la pensée...[10]

The specific rejection of reasoning is the principal factor creating a gulf between such a notion and Apollinaire's comparatively timid projection, 'Apollinaire n'ayant possédé ... que *la lettre*, encore imparfaite, du surréalisme et s'étant montré impuissant à en donner un aperçu théorique qui nous retienne' (ibid., p. 34). The poet whom Breton calls 'un "voyant" considérable' (see below, p. 122) attracted him by his attachment to the magus tradition and his claim to powers of prophecy as well as by his readiness to see poetry not simply in books but also in painting, films and city streets. He was, on the other hand, denounced for his attitude to the war and for such 'bourgeois' aspirations as the Prix Goncourt (for which *L'Hérésiarque et Cie* was a candidate) and the Légion d'honneur. His ghost long haunted the surrealists' camp and was never completely exorcised. If he was for Breton 'le dernier poète' it was because, according to surrealist dogma, the making of poetry as a craft was a thing of the past along with 'toute préoccupation esthétique ou morale'. He remained nonetheless 'a rallying point, sensitive to the modern evolution because of his contagious sense of liberty' (Balakian, p. 21).

If Apollinaire was unsure what to do with his freedom, this very uncertainty seems to have been an important part of his legacy. His appreciation of advertising hoardings reminds us of the necessary distinction in a writer between self-involvement and self-advertisement, and in his proneness to the latter he has seemingly condoned it in others. Apollinaire cannot of course be held responsible for all the journalistic, slack poets who clamour, heart on sleeve, for our attention, but he did nothing to stem the flood. (It is often forgotten that many of his innovations had been introduced earlier, by Max Jacob for example, just as his was not the first book on cubism—that honour goes jointly to Gleizes and Metzinger.) Yet in French-speaking countries at least the severe limits of his innovations are readily recognised. Empty experimentation can, in the context of other writers, be seen for what it is and at the same time the real prosodic versatility recognised as valid contributions to a continuing tradition. To a Frenchman traditional echoes unheard by the average foreigner form a ground bass to Apollinaire's poetry. But he sought a most eclectic readership: 'je voudrais qu'aimassent mes vers un boxeur nègre et américain, une impératrice de Chine, un journaliste boche, un peintre espagnol, une jeune femme de bonne race française, une jeune paysanne italienne et un officier anglais des Indes' (*O.C.*, iv, 681). What would survive so many transmogrifications? To what lowest common denominator would Apollinaire's poetry be thus reduced?

One decidedly international vogue which Apollinaire almost certainly renewed was for what is now called 'concrete poetry'.

Isidore Isou's 'lettrisme' carried the flame which sparked off manifestos by eugen gomringer, Pierre Garnier, Ian Hamilton Finlay and many others in the 1950s and early 1960s. An excerpt from gomringer's statement of 1954 will show how closely akin it is to its unacknowledged *belle époque* forebear (avoiding capital letters as Apollinaire avoided punctuation):

headlines, slogans, groups of sounds and letters give rise to forms which could be models for a new poetry just waiting to be taken up for meaningful use. the aim of the new poetry is to give poetry an organic function in society again, and in doing so to restate the position of the poet in society... so the new poem is simple and can be perceived visually as a whole as well as in its parts. it becomes an object to be both seen and used ... its objective element of play is useful to modern man, whom the poet helps through his special gift for this kind of play-activity ... it is a reality in itself and not a poem about something or other. the constellation is an invitation.[11]

The 'constellation' not only has affinities with the calligramme, it also admits a relationship with the typography of publicity which itself is often calligrammatic and where Apollinaire already found poetry. Pierre Garnier's 'spatialisme' continues to explore the visual impact of words, letters or signs grouped on a page and conceived as a source of energy. Radiation is displayed in many ways in an image (both poetic and visual) such as 'Soleil mystique' where from the central word 'soleil' many times repeated other words and their concepts are generated: 'île', 'sol', 'il', 'ils', 'œil', 'aile'.[12] The shaping of words in advertisements and pop art alike derives from similar techniques and shows the danger of trivialisation.

The publicity-conscious aspect of Apollinaire, counterbalanced in him by a secretive shyness guarding the poetic mysteries he sensed within himself, may give short-term benefits but probably damages and distorts our judgement of him as a poet. One may well be troubled therefore to see among critics a veritable industry operating on the basis of the talisman of Apollinaire's name and 'charisma'. The self-perpetuating (and often self-congratulatory) process of publicity which is concerned with an image seems at variance with an intellectual search for truth.

But no special plea need be entered for the aspect of

Apollinaire's poetry which, although quite unoriginal in itself, not only found a deep and moving response in him which he was able to verbalise in haunting images and rhythms but also rekindled for others the very essence of traditional French poetry: the lyric, often elegiac strain of so many of his best-loved and most-remembered pieces. The lyric and especially the amorous 'I' had rather faded in the shadow of the Parnassian school: the detached coolness of some, the scrupulous chiselling of other late nineteenth-century poets left room for a frank warm-hearted sentimentalist. Harking back to poets from Villon to Verlaine, Apollinaire almost certainly helped Eluard and Aragon to find their individual voices. But the list of possible names to adduce is scarcely subject to control: Apollinaire was a continuer, not an originator, of the lyrical and other traditions. Can any simple ballad of lost love be traced back to him? Do Yevtushenko's 'poèmes-conversations' owe anything to him? Is a tribute by Allen Ginsberg or Adrian Henri evidence of more than pygmies trying to climb on a giant's shoulders? The links of understanding and misunderstanding seem so tenuous that it would be wiser for us to return to a consideration of Apollinaire's poetry itself. Too changeable and elusive to head a school, he had so restless an imagination and involved himself so whole-heartedly in the *avant-garde* of his time that while he will continue to appeal to many as a shining example of modernity he will appal others who find poetry so betrayed by journalism.

One celebrated early review of *Alcools* by Georges Duhamel, reproduced with many others by Décaudin in his presentation of the critical reception given to the volume (*Dossier*, pp. 42–51), is hostile (except to 'Rhénanes' and isolated lines) but perceptive:

> Rien ne fait plus penser à une boutique de brocanteur que ce recueil de vers…
>
> …
>
> M. Apollinaire ne manque pas d'érudition; on a constamment l'impression qu'il dit tout ce qu'il sait. Aussi, brave-t-il impudemment les règles les plus accommodantes de la mesure et du goût. Deux idées, si distantes soient-elles dans le monde des réalités, sont toujours, pour le poète, liées par un fil secret et ténu. Il appartient au plus grand art de tendre ce fil jusqu'à sa limite d'élasticité; il appartient à l'ambition et à la maladresse de casser ce fil en voulant trop le tendre. Autrement dit,

plus une image s'adresse à des objets naturellement distants dans le temps et l'espace, plus elle est surprenante et suggestive. (*Dossier*, p. 49)

The last paragraph, apart from reminding us of 'Liens', the first poem in *Calligrammes*, looks forward with astonishing accuracy to the theory of the image formulated by Reverdy and propounded by Breton in the first *Manifeste du surréalisme* as a cornerstone of surrealist poetics:

L'image est une création pure de l'esprit.

Elle ne peut naître d'une comparaison mais du rapprochement de deux réalités plus ou moins éloignées.

Plus les rapports des deux réalités rapprochées seront lointains et justes, plus l'image sera forte—plus elle aura de puissance émotive et de réalité poétique...

A new 'querelle des anciens et des modernes' is here in a nutshell. Steering a course towards the true value of the poetry between the Scylla of conservatism and the Charybdis of modernism in a fog of factious, factitious publicity is a delicate task indeed.

ORDER AND ADVENTURE

At the outset of my analysis of Apollinaire's poetry, I used what is a commonplace of Apollinaire criticism by positing the polarity of order and adventure which he himself sets out in 'La Jolie Rousse'. That polarity may now be seen, after a study of his poetry, prose and criticism, as a far from simple one. There may well exist elements of adventure within order and of order within adventure, and these are likely to be features redeeming in the one case backward-looking unoriginality and in the other unfocussed experimentation.[1]

The pivotal moment in Apollinaire's output may be taken as a time in late 1912 when Delaunay helped him tip the balance from seeking adventure within order to seeking order within adventure. The poems nearest in spirit (and often nearest in time) to that turning-point of equilibrium or those given new shape or force under the new impulse are generally acknowledged to be his finest or most interesting works: the maturest achievements of *Alcools* on the one hand and 'Zone' and the first section of *Calligrammes* on the other. The first might, with some over-simplification, be classed as Apollinaire's achievement and the second what most generates excitement in his work.

The early years of this century are themselves often seen as pivotal between consolidation and discovery. France had enjoyed peace for a generation, colonial empires seemed to offer economic security, positivism had not really been unseated as the philosophy of social perfectibility, and among those who had means there was a comfortable self-righteousness. At the same time expansionist policies and leisured well-being created the atmosphere for scientific and artistic ferment of quite extraordinary intensity. These were the years of discoveries which revolutionised our view of the world, the years of Planck, Rutherford, Bohr and Einstein; revolutionised our view of man—Freud and Jung; revolutionised his communications—on roads, in the air, by wire and wireless; revolutionised his aesthetic environment—Debussy, Stravinsky, Schoenberg; Cézanne, Matisse, Picasso,

Braque, Kandinsky; Gide, Claudel and of course Apollinaire. He stands at the threshold of a new era and represents that fulcrum in a particularly complete way not because he invented more or more important things than the others named but because his uneasy balance between past and future suggests in one man's work the hidden tensions of the *belle époque*.

In his lyricism, his use of the alexandrine and other formal metres and fixed forms, ballad or song, in his appeal to folklore and fairy-tale, classical and Christian mythology, pastoral imagery and the timeless themes of unrequited love and fleeting time, Apollinaire looks back to a tradition he had striven to acquire in order to make himself ineradicably French. In his fragmentation of standard typography, his suppression of punctuation, in his use of relaxed free verse, of the stream-of-consciousness technique, of startling juxtapositions of reference and register, he strives to build on that acquired culture a literary personality of his own. It is ironic that through his lack of a clear aesthetic he neither resolved nor managed to maintain the valid tension between tradition and invention.

Lawrence of Arabia once said of T. S. Eliot that he was a *parvenu* longing for roots. The description fits Apollinaire like a glove. Even if nothing were known of his external biography, the fact would emerge from his writings. His over-compensation for being a foreigner is something we understand and forgive. Even late in his life he wrote, 'je suis quoique soldat et blessé, quoique volontaire, un naturalisé, tenu par conséquent à une très grande circonspection' (*O.C.*, iv, 885). The Mona Lisa affair had been a blunt reminder of his vulnerability in this respect. His justification, an entirely reasonable one which had many parallels in the cosmopolitan Paris of the pre-war years, seems to be voiced in the opening lines of his short story, 'Giovanni Moroni':

Il y a maintenant, comme en tous pays d'ailleurs, tant d'étrangers en France qu'il n'est pas sans intérêt d'étudier la sensibilité de ceux d'entre eux qui, étant nés ailleurs, sont cependant venus ici assez jeunes pour être façonnés par la haute civilisation française. Ils introduisent dans leur pays d'adoption les impressions de leur enfance, les plus vives de toutes, et enrichissent le patrimoine spirituel de leur nouvelle nation comme le chocolat et le café, par exemple, ont étendu le domaine du goût. (*O.C.*, i, 310)

Apollinaire's 'sensibilité' in searching for roots was also of course a tacit admission of rootlessness. His acquisition of French culture and particularly of its literature and language seems to stem from a laudable effort which gained such momentum that it continued well beyond the needs of original intentions, becoming an end in itself which had lost its *raison d'être*. If, in his work, we find so many echoes of or references to earlier writers, it is the literary form of that mimicry he found impossible to dominate in his everyday poses. His friend Fernand Fleuret's observations are particularly apposite:

Apollinaire cherchait, avant tout, à séduire. Ceux qui l'ont approché savent combien il y réussissait. Cependant, de tous les portraits que l'on a laissés de lui, aucun ne ressemble à l'autre, et bien peu sont les amis qui l'ont connu sous son vrai jour. C'est que, pour mieux plaire, il s'identifiait à son interlocuteur; il en pénétrait très rapidement les goûts et les pensées, il en prenait parfois les manières, et je lui ai même trouvé dans la journée plusieurs intonations ou façons de parler différentes, selon qu'il venait de s'entretenir avec les uns ou avec les autres... Vous retrouviez votre voix dans sa bouche, un peu de vos pensées dans les siennes, et quelquefois de vos lettres dans ses articles. J'ai toujours cru qu'il avait fait sa propre charge dans l'amusante nouvelle qui a pour titre la *Disparition d'Honoré Subrac*, et qui traite du mimétisme.[2]

Apollinaire's very histrionics betray an uncertainty at the centre of his personality. J.-Cl. Chevalier relates to specific poems what he terms 'cette angoisse coupable d'Apollinaire, ce sentiment de la négativité qui hante le poète d'*Alcools*'[3] and one can see that a man so absorbed in both past and future is faced with the very real existential problem of discovering his present, his identity. At the end of 'Le Poète assassiné' Apollinaire imagines a memorial which suggests that he recognised the truth of that fearful void:

—Il faut que je lui fasse une statue, dit l'oiseau du Bénin. Car je ne suis pas seulement peintre, mais aussi sculpteur.

—C'est ça, dit Tristouse, il faut lui élever une statue.

—Où ça? demanda l'oiseau du Bénin; le gouvernement ne nous accordera pas d'emplacement. Les temps sont mauvais pour les poètes.

—On le dit, répliqua Tristouse, mais ce n'est peut-être pas vrai. Que pensez-vous du bois de Meudon, monsieur l'oiseau du Bénin?

—J'y avais bien pensé, mais je n'osais le dire. Va pour le bois de Meudon.

—Une statue en quoi? demanda Tristouse. En marbre? En bronze?

—Non, c'est trop vieux, répondit l'oiseau du Bénin, il faut que je lui sculpte une profonde statue en rien, comme la poésie et comme la gloire.

—Bravo! bravo! dit Tristouse en battant des mains, une statue en rien, en vide, c'est magnifique, et quand la sculpterez-vous?

—Demain, si vous voulez; nous allons dîner, nous passerons la nuit ensemble, et dès le matin nous irons au bois de Meudon, où je sculpterai cette profonde statue. (*O.C.*, i, 294–5)

This 'profonde statue en rien, comme la poésie et comme la gloire' combines amusement and self-awareness (as well as passing jibes at Picasso and perhaps Marie Laurencin) to an astonishing degree, highlighting the paradox of Apollinaire's activities and very existence as a poet. Unable to define to his own satisfaction what he really meant by 'poésie' and the 'gloire' it brought with it in its wake, he escaped into humour, borrowed clothing or postures that would 'épater le bourgeois'.

One of the sources of his own confusion and certainly one of the critic's is the frequent coincidence of the literary 'I' with the real 'I'. While we may again agree with T. E. Lawrence that 'sincerity is the only written thing which time improves',[4] the distinction must be clearly maintained between 'real-life' sincerity—honesty to oneself about oneself—and the criteria appropriate for valid poetry, where sincerity which fails to respect the aesthetic forms of the medium is likely to generate self-indulgence at the expense of balance. As Michael Hamburger writes in *The Truth of Poetry* (p. 88), 'the first person in lyrical poetry serves to convey a gesture, not to document identity or establish biographical facts. Only when poets forget this does the first person become "egotistical" and usually boring as well'.

If we feel Apollinaire not to have been equal to the struggle within himself between order and adventure, the task of the literary critic should be to suggest where this inadequacy shows in his poetry. It is not sufficient to approach the work with preconceived reactionary or radical principles and prejudices and consequently dismiss too easily one whole area of the complex totality of Apollinaire. My own view is that the vast majority of his poetry falls between two stools: the overlap between achievement and excitement is remarkably small, and our attention is therefore, on Apollinaire's invitation, drawn towards an alluring human being and away from his literary creations. The excitement of experiments such as those which crowd into 'Ondes', the first section of *Calligrammes*, is manifest. The sheer variety of formal presentation is stimulus enough, from the unrhymed octosyllabic *quintils* of 'Les Collines', through *vers libres* to the calligrammes: 'il ne peut y avoir aujourd'hui de lyrisme authentique sans la liberté complète du poète et même s'il écrit en vers réguliers c'est sa liberté qui le convie à ce jeu; hors de cette liberté il ne saurait plus y avoir de poésie' (*O.C.*, iv, 676). In fact he never took his formal experiments further than he did here. The juxtaposition of different times and preoccupations in 'a day in the life of Guillaume Apollinaire' in 'Zone' is condensed further in such a 'poème-conversation' as 'Lundi rue Christine' where disjunction is given positive value and formlessness becomes a legitimate type of form. Yet do we not value 'Liens', 'Les Fenêtres' and 'Lundi rue Christine' more highly than the other pieces in the section not simply because they are experimental but because they achieve their own unity, their own integrity on their own terms? There is in each poem a reduction of irrelevant and gratuitous material, even in the extreme case of the 'poème-conversation', which gives formal appropriateness to the works as a whole. Such appropriateness is also present in the most obvious way in the calligrammes where word and picture (re-)present the same thing. But they are facile and parade in a limbo between drawing and literature. It is where Apollinaire assimilates the idea behind the calligrammes into purely verbal form that he provides himself with the basic structure for success. The total inevitability of true poetry is an important criterion. At his best, Apollinaire achieved this and recognised it in others: then one may apply to him what he wrote of a now forgotten composer: 'Son art s'efforce à capter toute la poésie qui jaillit des choses présentes. Son artifice s'emploie à nous les présenter sous *une forme fatidique*. Mais c'est surtout l'imagination qui l'élève' (*O.C.*, iv, 384; italics added). Active poetic mimesis must be distinguished from the ventriloquist's mimicry, and again it was a distinction Apollinaire did not always make.

Apollinaire did not have much poetic stamina. His real talent was for short pieces where the structural basis was readily governed by a particular image or single idea. 'Le Pont Mirabeau', 'Les Colchiques', 'Saltimbanques' and other successful lyrics represent as it were a single glance, putting little strain on either poet or reader. Genuine achievements, they show what Apollinaire could master completely and effortlessly—the real effort having preceded the production of the poems themselves. But he had ambitions to write more substantial pieces, and just as in prose his talent for the short story proved hopelessly inadequate to the composition of a novel ('Le Poète assassiné' and *La Femme assise* being Apollinaire's hapless attempts in the genre), so he aimed at the long dramatised confessional lyric of 'La Chanson du mal-aimé' and 'Zone'. The former, originally composed in 1903 according to the epigraph but probably given its final form with the striking interpolations not long before its first appearance in 1909, is doubtless sprawling and unintelligible in many details but nonetheless seems to achieve, by its balance of 'romance' and daring, an excitement within achievement, an adventure within order that retains its appeal. Some would say the same of 'Zone'. I suggest however that it lies to the other side of the scales, that it attempts order within adventure, achievement within excitement, and that while pointing a way forward it lacks a sufficient principle of coherence to make it totally satisfactory. By and large, then, one might say that poems of real aesthetic adventure ('Zone' and 'Ondes') generate excitement but remain pioneering (and in that sense unfulfilled), whereas those where the greatest sense of mastery and achievement is felt are those in which a traditional order is maintained. Apollinaire's relative failure as a poet may be measured by his failure to sustain the coincidence of the two principles of order and adventure.

He recognised in theory, for example, the unwisdom of following fashion and the limitation of journalism, writing of one contemporary: 'Il est décidément le poète à la mode, ce qui est souvent une façon d'être démodé' (*O.C.*, iv, 140), or saying of a minor painter: 'On peut même craindre qu'il ne soit atteint de ce mal moderne qui fait prendre comme but unique de l'art l'expression de la vie contemporaine' (ibid., 110). His belief in poetry and in his own position as a latter-day Orpheus was absolute: 'Je sais que ceux qui se livrent au travail de la poésie font quelque chose d'essentiel, de primordial, de nécessaire avant toute chose, quelque chose enfin de divin' (*Lettres à Lou*, p. 120). Yet it ill befits the magus to try leaping on every band-wagon that passes, as Apollinaire tended to do. Is it not rather the feat and feature of the sad clown? If there was something pathological about Apollinaire's search for roots, is there not also something pathetic about his humour? Is it not another thin veneer over the void he knew and feared within him? For the laugh rings hollow and camaraderie can be a measure taken to avoid too much introspection and, paradoxically, a way of preventing other people from probing and perhaps wounding too deeply. Wit and word-play are apparent throughout Apollinaire's work and his zest for life and language shows in the gamut from gross buffoonery to the subtlest irony. While it represents a refusal to be pinned down, each mask replaces another so rapidly that the real face scarcely shows and we become unsure of its existence. Attitudinising for Proteus is a form of protection.

Utterly different defences were necessary in the war when Apollinaire's fierce patriotism (which not even Breton doubted) came to the fore. It is a further complication to the paradox that Apollinaire seemed most at ease, most himself when far from the literary and artistic milieu he frequented before 1914. Perhaps the need to scintillate, a need which he had obviously felt and responded to, disappeared in the company of soldiers under a sinister threat well removed from the salons. His attitudes become far more consistent and are expressed in recurrent images not so much borrowed from others as drawn from the situation Apollinaire himself was experiencing. Formal experimentation goes no further but capitalises on pre-war variety; a gain in consistency is accompanied by a limitation in range. It is as if Apollinaire were living out those clangorous phrases from the 1909 Futurist manifesto by Marinetti which he had at first ignored, then flirted with and finally partly assimilated: 'We are out to glorify War—the only healthgiver of the world—Militarism, Patriotism, the Destructive arm of the Anarchist, Ideas that kill ... Poetry must be a violent onslaught. There is no masterpiece without aggressiveness'. Louis Allen makes this point and suggests a further reason why it is inappropriate to berate Apollinaire for his attitude to the war:

> We tend to take up a moralising attitude towards Apollinaire's poems on the First World War. The reason is quite simple: we have grown accustomed to seeing it as the unremitting filth and horror that it was, and therefore prefer poets who share that view, or who propounded it first. So Owen, Sassoon and Rosenberg appear to us as the 'correct stance' of any poet when faced by that filth and horror.
> But this does not arise from Apollinaire's lack of sensitivity. We have to see him, not as the prophet of a pacifist age, as the others were, but as the continuing voice of Futurism, for which war was a real and valuable manifestation of the new poetry of modern urban industrial life. In this sense, Apollinaire was deriving from war a vision perfectly consistent with that of Marinetti in the Futurist manifesto of 1909, in which war is one of the elements of modern life most strongly evoked as part of the new vision. So 'Merveilles de la guerre' is not ironic. These are *real* wonders, whatever the moral implications of them in suffering may be, as drawn out by other poets and novelists.[5]

If we are surprised, even shocked, by Apollinaire's lyrical shellbursts, it is only one of the surprises his poetry offers. Long before 1917 and 'L'Esprit nouveau et les poètes' he had practised the techniques of surprise in his work. His eclectic and disorderly erudition no less than his constant dissatisfaction with his achievements lent itself to unusual juxtapositions and presentations. That they were sometimes undigested or facile betrays his lack of critical discernment but is unlikely to deter new generations of readers from discovering features which are as startling and 'modern' today as they were at the time of first publication. Once discovered, they no doubt lose some of their impact—'le lyrisme doit se renouveler avec chaque génération' (*O.C.*, iv, 103)—but retain the aura that a first love might have in a mature person's memory. Just such a sensitive if sentimental person might respond favourably too to Apollinaire's parallel turn of mind and phrase. For Apollinaire's best-loved (if not his most demanding) poems are those in which he casts a sadly reflective eye on some mental suffering generally caused by an amorous relationship turning sour. He catches this autumnal mood with unerring accuracy if not always with equal felicity.

Critical images of Apollinaire are so varied that it is as if each reader fills the void in his own way. Yet if Apollinaire was suggestible he is also multiply suggestive. Like the paintings of the cubists he befriended, he is a simultaneous multiplicity of facets. Yet because he reflects so many influences, I see him rather as a broken mirror, precariously held together in its frame, longing to be resilvered and made whole. For in his quest for a new order incorporating the innovations of his time into the perspective of his acquired culture, he stands ironically as a landmark in the fragmentation of that culture. Had he been a real prophet he would have foreseen the cataclysmic difference that the First World War would make to European life. The background of humanistic values which he could afford to take for granted would no longer apply. Even his championing of non-verbal poetry would assume an ironic twist in that the poetic language which he so honoured would become devalued and literature be made to serve non-literary ends.

Most recent criticism has rightly and helpfully concentrated on Apollinaire's literature as a value in itself. Formalist and structuralist studies have analysed many a poem and shown how it works on its own terms just as thematic and phenomenological criticism has helped define the preoccupations of Apollinaire's imagination, showing how the sun, food, eyes and fire, for example, had particular significance for him. Such studies tend by their very methodology, however, to presuppose or ignore value judgements which it is nonetheless an important function of criticism to try and establish. Because of his own extreme positions, Apollinaire lends himself to extreme judgements. And because of the evident power of his personality and his association with a brilliant group of artists, many a reader has been seduced by the anecdotal away from the more taxing but more rewarding analysis of the poetry. Yet it is in the poetry, if anywhere, that we are going to find reasons why Apollinaire has lasting value. If we explain a reference by an incident, we elude the poetry and delude ourselves. And if we say explicitly or implicitly that the man is more interesting than his poetry, do we not condemn the poet for failing in his task?

Replying to a criticism of his short stories, Apollinaire wrote:

Ces négligences sont la seule chose qui me chagrine, car pour la personnalité, elle est le dernier de mes soucis, la perfection étant le seul but que doive, à mon sens, se proposer l'écrivain. La personnalité domine sans qu'on le veuille, et je crains que les principaux défauts de mon livre ne proviennent d'elle. (*O.C.*, iv, 752)

This laudable goal of perfection and of that abstraction of the personality which allows the kind of sincerity which time improves was too absolute for Apollinaire's own practice (and indeed one wonders to what extent his tongue was in his cheek when writing the above). A more realistic aim which he sometimes managed most memorably to achieve is expressed as adventure within order: 'La meilleure façon d'être classique et pondéré est d'être de son temps en ne sacrifiant rien de ce que les Anciens ont pu nous apprendre' (ibid., 675), or as order within adventure: 'C'est en encourageant l'audace et en tempérant la témérité que l'on réalise l'ordre' (ibid., 423).

Poetry is not a matter of competition: a man is a true poet or not. That Apollinaire claimed poetic powers need not influence our judgement: he has to prove them in practice. Nor need any reader's opinion of that practice be considered in any way definitive, the more so given Apollinaire's Protean nature. The selection of points of view printed after this chapter, the bibliography and suggestions for further reading are all intended to provoke further thought and discussion towards the formulation of informed personal views. But I shall have failed in my main task if my reader is not now prompted to return to Apollinaire's poetry itself to explore or ponder afresh on its varied and elusive qualities, self-contradictory, inspiring, infuriating, more tragic for being more complex, more magic for being more simple.

POINTS OF VIEW

(N.B. Full details of sources are given only where the item does not figure in the bibliography or suggestions for further reading at the end of this volume.)

Rien ne fait plus penser à une boutique de brocanteur que ce recueil de vers ... [*Alcools*].

Je dis: boutique de brocanteur parce qu'il est venu échouer dans ce taudis une foule d'objets hétéroclites dont certains ont de la valeur, mais dont aucun n'est le produit de l'industrie du marchand même. C'est bien là une des caractéristiques de la brocante: elle revend; elle ne fabrique pas. Elle revend d'ailleurs parfois de curieuses choses; il se peut qu'on trouve, dans ses étalages crasseux, une pierre de prix montée sur un clou. Tout cela vient de loin; mais la pierre est agréable à voir. Pour le reste, c'est un assemblage de faux tableaux, de vêtements exotiques et rapiécés, d'accessoires pour bicyclettes et d'instruments d'hygiène privée. Une truculente et étourdissante variété tient lieu d'art, dans l'assemblage des objets.

> Georges Duhamel, reviewing *Alcools*, *Mercure de France*, 16 June 1913. See also above pp. 107–8.

... il se pourrait que Duhamel, bien malgré lui, ait rendu à Apollinaire l'hommage non le plus chaleureux, certes, mais le plus exact ... Car enfin ne tenons-nous pas là une des caractéristiques majeures de la poésie d'Apollinaire, dès l'abord sensible au lecteur, mais plus sensible encore au critique qui se plaît à retrouver ici un souvenir d'enfance, là une réminiscence littéraire, ailleurs une citation de l'auteur ou d'un de ses amis, plus loin une impression saisie au vol, regret d'hier ou pressentiment de son destin, le détail d'un visage ou d'un tableau, des bribes de rêves ou de conversations, que sais-je encore?—mais tout cela parfaitement unifié en un ton qui ne trompe pas.

> Jean Burgos, 'Pour une approche de l'univers imaginaire d'Apollinaire', *RLM* (GA), 10, 1971, p. 38.

In everything he showed himself to be a strange mixture of not completely integrated opposites, still precariously poised between them, as on a rope bridge between opposing peaks. Still trying to push forward, still wanting to live every moment to the full, still grasping at every opportunity, he made, like every opportunist, some moves which might have seemed silly, but some also which were strategically sound.

> Margaret Davies, *Apollinaire*, p. 169.

Humain ... il l'était avec toutes les contradictions que cela suppose: tendresse et gros rire, finesse du cœur et gaillardise, goût et mauvais goût, poésie exigeante et poésie facile, art et journalisme, classicisme et baroque. Nul n'a mieux ouvert l'avenir, nul n'a été plus authentiquement prophète et nul n'a été plus "contingent", plus dépendant de son époque.

> Raymond Jean, 'Lire et relire Apollinaire', *Le Monde*, 22 October 1966.

Plus que quiconque aujourd'hui il a tracé des routes neuves, ouvert de nouveaux horizons. Il a droit à toute notre ferveur, toute notre admiration.

> Pierre Reverdy, *Nord-Sud*, No. 1, 1917.

Il n'a cure d'une doctrine logiquement et continûment déduite. Bonhomme, malin, ou exalté, il pense par éclairs d'images. Insaisissables les ombres devant lui se nouent et se dénouent, la flamme est torsion, tournoiement, ou tremblement, et rien n'est plus rapide qu'elle, sinon la mémoire qui ressuscite les morts. Mais pourchasseur des fantômes de nuées, et des fumées comme des fusées, "mélodieux ravisseur", tzigane amoureux, langoureux flûtiste, modulateur sentimental, essayeur inventif de nouveautés insolites, amant du hasard, virtuose négligent et amusé plein d'abandon et de laisser-aller, il a été aussi théoricien agressif, et surtout candidat-mage. Il a su par instants donner à la poésie le haut ton du plus fier lyrisme, et, d'autres fois, il a mis en elle réflexion, méditation, philosophie, métaphysique, à sa manière ambiguë, enveloppée, flottante, un peu molle. Il lui arrive même d'être guetté par l'intellectualisme. Mais l'attaque de l'image le sauve toujours, la prise de la pensée dans l'image.

Poète né, en qui la pensée n'est pas distincte du pouvoir imaginant ou de la rêverie.

> Marie-Jeanne Durry, *Guillaume Apollinaire: 'Alcools'*, iii, pp. 208-9.

With Apollinaire, the writing of poetry was only one of a wide variety of activities, which he pursued with an erratic brilliance. He was above all an experimenter ... Apollinaire's achievements, like those of the Surrealists who claimed him as their immediate predecessor, are less impressive than his intentions. His work is extraordinarily mixed and uneven, but in it there are individual verses, refrains, and short lyrics which have more than a period interest. He is at his best, not when he is striving to be modern, nor when he is prophesying about the future of poetry, but when he is drawing strength from traditional sources. His most successful work is, in fact, that which reflects the work of other and greater poets, such as Villon, Rimbaud and Verlaine.

> C. A. Hackett, *An Anthology of Modern French Poetry: From Baudelaire to the Present Day*, Oxford: Blackwell, 3rd edn, 1967, pp. 280-1.

La poésie moderne, ce n'est pas Apollinaire. Avant lui, c'est Max Jacob; après c'est Dada et André Breton.

> Michel Pierssens, 'Apollinaire, Picasso et la mort de la poésie', *Europe*, Nos 492-3 (April-May 1970), p. 189.

... si son œuvre le montre souvent merveilleusement sensible au lyrisme épars dans la vie, il ne s'est pas avancé très loin, il n'est pas allé jusqu'à mettre en question par la poésie l'existence même... la poésie est pour lui l'expression de la vie, non la promesse de sa transformation, le lieu d'un appel bouleversant et insaisissable. Il cherche de nouveaux domaines pour l'art, non un élargissement de la connaissance; il ambitionne une expression plus totale du réel, non son agrandissement, alors que les surréalistes transformeront la notion même du réel ...

> Marguerite Bonnet, 'Aux sources du surréalisme: place d'Apollinaire', *RLM* (GA), 3, 1964, p. 71.

... dès le début de la période représentée par *Calligrammes*, la poésie d'Apollinaire est axée sur la notion de création poétique. Pour lui le rôle du poète n'est plus simplement d'exprimer ses sentiments intimes: dans un monde où les changements les plus rapides se succèdent, et où d'autres créateurs—les peintres au premier chef—ont bouleversé toutes les formes admises de leur art, le poète doit, lui aussi, créer du nouveau.

C'est sur le plan de la structure que cette notion trouve sa première application dans son œuvre. Pour être à la hauteur d'une époque fertile en surprises et en renouvellements, le poète doit créer des formes qui ne sont pas moins capables de frapper et d'étonner... Très vite, la même attitude se fait jour sur le plan de l'image poétique elle-même.

> S. I. Lockerbie, 'Le Rôle de l'imagination dans *Calligrammes*, 2e partie: Les Poèmes du monde intérieur', *RLM* (GA), 6, 1967, p. 85.

Qu'on l'accuse de rouerie, de naïveté, de vulgarité, peu importe. Il sera le poète des "choses neuves", de la Tour Eiffel et des express, des enseignes lumineuses et de la vitesse, de la quotidienneté de la rue, du jazz et de l'écran. A l'exemple des premiers aventuriers de l'air qui, sur leurs fragiles et risibles machines, amorcent la conquête du cosmos, il se situera, lui, en tant que chantre lyrique de la modernité au-dessus de toutes les frontières, y compris celles de l'espace et du temps.

> Georges Dupeyron, 'Espace et temps dans la poésie de Guillaume Apollinaire', *Europe*, Nos. 451–2 (November-December 1966), p. 194.

Il était ... l'apôtre de cette conception qui exige de tout nouveau poème qu'il soit une refonte totale des moyens de son auteur, qu'il coure son aventure propre hors des chemins déjà tracés, au mépris des gains réalisés antérieurement ... Il fut un "voyant" considérable.

> André Breton, from *Entretiens* in *Les Critiques de notre temps et Apollinaire*, pp. 18–19. From radio interview of 1952.

Peu s'en faut qu'on ne croie découvrir, dans chacun de ses poèmes, un nouveau poète. Où le saisir? Sur le champ de sa pensée, dès qu'on veut l'éclairer, s'accumulent tous les nuages. On est réduit à faire des conjectures sur ses préférences intimes, sur la valeur qu'il attribuait lui-même à ses tentatives. D'ailleurs, sa paresse, son manque de persévérance, rendent ses intentions douteuses. Il faut aussi compter avec son besoin de mystifier, bien qu'il ait dit souvent: il n'y a que moi qui sois sincère.

Marcel Raymond, *De Baudelaire au surréalisme*, p. 229.

A une époque où la poésie est souvent prisonnière des systèmes et des théories, Apollinaire a su être simplement poète. Simplement, mais totalement: ne refusant rien de ce que lui apporte le monde, unissant dans un même embrassement spectacle de la vie, expérience personnelle et culture, accueillant toutes les formes de l'expression poétique, sensible à tous les appels esthétiques de son temps, sauvegardant par un accent inimitable la pureté de son inspiration au cœur de sollicitations multiples.

Michel Décaudin, *Le Dossier d'"Alcools"*, p. 63.

Guillaume Apollinaire represented primarily the irresponsible side of his period and was blind to some of its most important features. Yet he had an intuition of its complexity and was aware of living in an age of far-reaching changes. If their nature sometimes escaped him, as was inevitable, he fought for them in his fashion, which may now seem somewhat old-fashioned. To be in turns jumpy, pathetic, humorous, imitative and original was his temperamental limitation; but it also qualifies him to represent a particular point in time better than any other poet.

...

The reputation which he has left is that of an innovator and to a large extent it is justified. Discarding extravagant claims made on his behalf to be considered as the father of modern poetry, one can at least regard him as one of its most amusing and versatile uncles.

...

Apollinaire was rightly regarded in his early days as a young poet who was continuing Symbolism. It was the first stage in his search for a poetic identity which he never completely found. His break-out from the traditional verse-form, which seems to constitute his strongest claim to originality, was a continuation of that search and its fruits were willed; they were not the product of any deep emotional, or aesthetic impulsion.

...

To sum up Apollinaire briefly is impossible because of his

diversity. In some writers this is an outstanding virtue because it stems from a passionate exploration of the various means by which truth as they conceive it can be attained. But it is hard to detect any passion of this kind in Apollinaire's shifts of ground or any development in his art which can be related to an inner compulsion. Nor is it easy to know what ends he was seeking, except notoriety and stability. On the level on which Apollinaire pursued them, neither of these absolutely necessitates poetry... He remains as a copious if shallow source of ideas and rhythms —particularly to free-verse poets—as the author of a number of hauntingly simple verses in an older manner, and as a foil to such monolithic figures as Claudel, Péguy and Romain Rolland... His liking for the inconsequential, and the fact that he apparently 'suffers' but refuses to labour his suffering, have kept him attuned to a trend in modern French poetry whose importance is undeniable. His technical experiments have also proved surprisingly fruitful and, this being so, the spirit in which he undertook them matters far less than the results.

Geoffrey Brereton, *An Introduction to the French Poets: Villon to the Present Day*, London: Methuen, 2nd edn 1973, pp. 247–55.

... nous vivons le siècle Apollinaire. On s'en apercevra plus tard.

Max Jacob, *Les Nouvelles littéraires*, 23 February 1935.

Enfin Apollinaire, le poète Guillaume Apollinaire trouve, en son temps, la hauteur interdite à tout autre que lui, et trace la nouvelle voie lactée entre le bonheur, l'esprit et la liberté, triangle en exil dans le ciel de la poésie de notre siècle tragique, tandis que des labeurs pourtant bien distincts, en activité partout, se promettent d'établir, avec de la réalité éprouvée, *une cité* encore jamais aperçue sous l'emblème de la lyre.

René Char, 'La Conversation souveraine' in *Recherche de la base et du sommet*, Gallimard, Coll. Poésie, 1971, p. 121. First published 1953.

... il est indéniable qu'Apollinaire s'est entendu mieux que tout autre à faire passer dans l'expression, seul domaine où il excellait, quelques-unes des attitudes les plus caractéristiques de l'humour d'aujourd'hui. Si ce sens lui a fait radicalement défaut dans tels cas de la vie où entre tous il eût été de circonstance ... c'est à merveille qu'il a su le faire passer dans ses poèmes et dans ses contes... C'est au terme même de sa volonté de libération de tous les genres littéraires que, porté poétiquement par un vent furieux, dans l'éperdu de l'imagination seule, il lui est arrivé de rencontrer le grand humour.

André Breton, *Anthologie de l'humour noir*, Livre de poche, 1970, pp. 310–11. First published 1940.

C'est dans [le] milieu des humoristes qu'il faut replacer Guillaume Apollinaire... Mais sa jeunesse des aventures plus profondes ...; il en tira les poèmes d'*Alcools*, imponctués, déréglés, disparates, burlesques et souvent impénétrables, mais d'où émergeaient la *Chanson du mal aimé*, *Le Pont Mirabeau* et, çà et là, des gammes admirables de musique grelottante et de poésie pure. Par un plaisant paradoxe, ce novateur inégal n'est à la cime de sa poésie qu'aux instants où, délaissant toute prétention d'élévation sublime ou d'épiphanie futuriste, il n'écoute que son cœur, sa sensibilité naïve mariée à une imagination truculente.

...

Le meilleur témoignage venu du front, c'est sans doute à Guillaume Apollinaire que nous le devons: il reste, dans *Calligrammes*, une fois écartées les prétentieuses recherches typographiques qui transformaient le poème en idéogramme, un franc impressionnisme, un mélange de pitié contenue et de bonne humeur virile, avec des élans vrais de sentimentalité amoureuse et de rêveries sensuelles; là, les manières de vivre et de sentir de l'homme des tranchées de Champagne se reflétaient en bonne poésie.

Pierre-Henri Simon, *Histoire de la littérature française au XXe siècle*, Paris: Armand Colin, 3e tirage, 1967, i, pp. 107, 116.

Des petits Français, moitié anglais, moitié nègre, moitié russe, un
   peu belge, italien, annamite, tchèque
L'un a l'accent canadien, l'autre les yeux hindous
Dents face os jointures galbe démarche sourire
Ils ont tous quelque chose d'étranger et sont pourtant bien de
   chez nous
Au milieu d'eux, Apollinaire, comme cette statue du Nil, le père
   des eaux, étendu avec des gosses qui lui coulent de partout

Entre les pieds, sous les aisselles, dans la barbe
Ils ressemblent à leur père et se départent de lui
Et ils parlent tous la langue d'Apollinaire

Paris, novembre 1918.
Blaise Cendrars, 'Hommage à Guillaume Apollinaire' in *Poèmes divers* in *Poésies complètes*, Denoël, 1963, p. 192.

Pour lui le lyrisme n'était pas l'expression de sentiments personnels, ni le cri d'une conscience isolée dans le monde; c'était l'exercice d'un pouvoir magique, dans une perspective de nature orphique et prométhéenne; un exercice sacré, lié au rêve millénaire de l'agrandissement de la conscience, des pouvoirs spirituels de l'humanité... On aurait tort de voir dans 'Zone' l'exaltation de la vie et de la ville modernes. Ce qu'Apollinaire y cherche, ce n'est pas le modernisme, c'est la jeunesse... Il est remarquable qu'Apollinaire n'aime du monde moderne, dans 'Zone', que les symboles d'un bonheur perdu... Mais ce poème n'est pas inspiré par une nouvelle esthétique. Il marque plutôt le renoncement à toute idée préconçue de la poésie et du poète.

Philippe Renaud, *Lecture d'Apollinaire*, pp. 33, 94, 96.

Zone and *La Chanson du mal-aimé* are self-discoveries rather than self-projections...

As a poet who looked back as much as he looked forward, who vacillated between a Futuristic delight in anything that was new and a weary longing for that 'ceremony of innocence' which many of the twentieth-century innovations served to 'drown', Apollinaire had no need to emphasise his representative status. His very desire to be a representative figure and to combine 'perfection of the life' with 'perfection of the work' was strangely anachronistic, more reminiscent of Victor Hugo than of Hugo's successors. It was also a naïve ambition; and the same naïveté that makes Apollinaire so attractive a character accounts for many of his shortcomings as a poet—his tendency to plagiarize, for instance, or his inability to resist conventional rhetoric and lyricism of a kind not truly compatible with his equally genuine passion for modernity.

...

As often as not Apollinaire's false steps as a poet were obeisances to conventions and orders which he was not adventurous enough to leave behind, and it is these lapses that account for many impurities of diction, structure and gesture in his poetry. For all his enthusiastic championing of a succession of modernist movements, even Apollinaire's manifestos and critical essays show that his break with Romantic–Symbolist practices was a restoration as much as it was a revolution.

...

Apollinaire's basic naïveté—maintained despite much that is 'cerebral', deliberate and 'faux-naïf' in his work—redeems many of his lapses, even in the sequences of love and war poems written towards the end of his life.

> Michael Hamburger, *The Truth of Poetry: Tensions in Modern Poetry from Baudelaire to the 1960s*, pp. 184–92.

Apollinaire was above all a lyric poet, and the bulk of his verse is in the first person. The elusiveness of the self and the emotions it excites constitute a dominant theme. Indeed he was one of the first and the most lucid among the hordes of writers—and readers—engaged in the search for their indefinable identities in this twentieth century.

His rootlessness generated an exhilarating sense of freedom. He felt bound by no traditions, no taboos... But non-involvement can weigh heavily, and just as often we find him thirsting after more binding ties... Such oscillation in turn reveals a deeper trait in Apollinaire: his congenital indecisiveness. Coming from no direction, he knew not what direction to go.

> LeRoy C. Breunig, *Guillaume Apollinaire*, pp. 6–7.

Si l'élégie se définit au poème d'une inspiration triste et tendre, si le meilleur d'Apollinaire, ce qui nous touche de plus en lui, ce qui a fait sa popularité, relève de l'élégie ainsi conçue, Apollinaire a été notre dernier élégiaque.

> André Billy, Preface to Apollinaire, *Œuvres poétiques*, p. xlvi.

Avec *Alcools*, Apollinaire publie un poème du temps, avec *Calligrammes* un poème de l'espace. Il n'y a pas seulement entre *Alcools* et *Calligrammes* une différence de thème, mais aussi de qualité: l'un restant une expérience uniquement littéraire du temps sacré (ce qui explique peut-être et sa réussite et son succès auprès des lecteurs), l'autre étant l'ébauche du journal d'une expérience vécue, d'une pénétration réelle de l'espace sacré.

Jean Roudaut, 'L'Espace sacré' in *Les Critiques de notre temps et Apollinaire*, p. 102.

L'auteur d'*Alcools* n'est pas exactement ce qu'on appelle un érudit; malgré sa réputation flatteuse dans ce domaine, ... il emprunte à l'érudition ses moyens mais non ses fins. Nous verrions plutôt en lui un explorateur ou un alchimiste.

Marc Poupon, *Apollinaire et Cendrars*, Paris: Minard, 1969, p. 44.

Apollinaire regarde vers l'arrière tout en croyant de bonne foi annoncer l'avenir. C'est le fait d'un langage prisonnier de lui-même et de ses connotations, et qui véhicule avec lui—qu'il s'agisse de poésie ou de critique—des concepts inadéquats aux nouvelles réalités, et fonde l'illusion d'une communauté d'intentions et de visions sur les ambiguïtés d'un discours irrémédiablement impropre à servir son objet.

Michel Pierssens, 'Apollinaire, Picasso, et la mort de la poésie', *Europe*, Nos. 492–3 (April–May 1970), p. 187.

The sense of alienation and the search for identity in Apollinaire's work have a peculiar flavour which sets him apart from other writers who have treated the same theme. When he writes in 'Zone' of 'la grâce de cette rue industrielle' he is unselfconsciously celebrating the joys and pleasures of being alive which never deserted him, even in his blackest moments... For Apollinaire the world is good and it is he, the 'poète maudit', who cannot share its pleasures... Apollinaire does not wish to change the world but rather to make its joys and mysteries available to all.

Garnet Rees, 'Guillaume Apollinaire and the Search for Identity' in *Order and Adventure in Post-Romantic French Poetry: Essays presented to C. A. Hackett*, p. 173.

[In 'Zone'] le poète n'a donc pu s'évader d'un univers souillé, il y retombe sans rémission: d'une putain à l'autre, tel est le cycle lamentable! L'évocation des paradis: celui d'un monde neuf dans la lumière du soleil, celui de l'enfance aux virginales couleurs, celui de la religion chrétienne, ne fait que rendre plus amère cette rechute dans l'existence quotidienne qui est un enfer.

Un enfer social, celui des malheureux: émigrants, pauvres, Juifs, prostituées;—déracinés, *heimatlose, outlaws,* que leur aliénation peut conduire au vice, voire au crime—comme le disait nettement la forme originelle de la séquence consacrée aux malheureux. ("Rien ne pousse au mal que de n'avoir pas d'argent.") Compatissant, *souffrant avec* les malheureux, Apollinaire dénonce ainsi, en cette séquence, la tare radicale du "monde ancien" fondé sur l'injustice et le mépris du pauvre.

Wilhelm de Kostrowitzki, qualifié de Juif, de métèque par des gens en place, s'insère naturellement "parmi les malheureux du jour et de la nuit". Il se sent lié à eux par de profondes racines, et, plus même que par une communauté de malheur, par une relation de race …

… 'Zone' … exorcise l'angoisse dont il est empli… [Dans le premier poème d'*Alcools*] apparaît l'Apollinaire franc païen qu'il était peut-être par tempérament, marqué, cependant, par sa première éducation, d'une empreinte difficile à effacer, dont 'Zone' opère la liquidation.

Robert Couffignal, *'Zone' d'Apollinaire: structure et confrontations,* pp. 20–2.

Dans la transposition des images visuelles en images affectives, dans la transformation du réel en allusion, de l'allusion au monde extérieur en allusion à la vie cachée, je sens un des secrets non plus de l'existence mais de la poésie d'Apollinaire. Plus précisément, un double secret de son art de conteur en poésie. L'un: prendre pour sujet l'anecdote, avec ses détails colorés, nets, presque tangibles, et la volatiliser. L'autre: raconter sans donner le mot du conte… Apollinaire dans *Alcools* cède sans cesse à la douceur de se raconter et pourtant préserve ses mystères … cet homme ostensible est un homme très caché … Sous des apparences exubérantes, il est fermé et de peu de confidences.

Marie-Jeanne Durry, *Guillaume Apollinaire: 'Alcools',* iii, pp. 29–30.

Il avait une véritable religion sensuelle et sentimentale à l'égard des femmes. Il y apportait aussi le sel d'un cynisme secret et d'un fond de barbarie imaginative, dont il savait s'irriter lui-même à la fois et rire. Les femmes l'ont toujours beaucoup préoccupé et, incessamment blessé au cœur par elles, toujours il y revenait à ces belles trompeuses qu'il attirait dès l'abord par son allégresse pensive... Fascinant à la fois et apeurant aux pucelles; attractif et enviable aux mieux expérimentées, et qui reconnaissaient en lui l'homme des grands remous du large, le pirate audacieux, barbare, sensible et, de cœur, sentimentalement, inaltérablement ingénu, encore qu'il ne laissait pas d'avoir la main prompte à l'occasion, ce qui, au demeurant, à l'épreuve, ne gâtait rien.

André Rouveyre, *Amour et poésie d'Apollinaire*, Seuil, 1955, pp. 196-7.

... rien ne lui est plus pénible que l'impression d'être *mal aimé*; il n'est pas de ces lutteurs qu'excitent obstacles et oppositions; il est une âme sensible (l'émotion tempérée par l'ironie) qui aime toute chose et a besoin de l'universelle sympathie.

Michael Décaudin, 'Pour un portrait d'Apollinaire', *O.C.*, i, p. 21.

Apollinaire nous dit sans cesse l'avenir en travail dans l'esprit humain... Ce cosmopolite ne se connaît d'autres frontières que celles de "l'illimité et de l'avenir". Il ne sait pas se restreindre. Les conceptions poétiques les plus aventureuses l'enthousiasment. "C'est qu'elles lui paraissent, dit Marcel Raymond, devoir fournir des matériaux pour un nouveau réalisme." ... Les concessions d'un poète géant à la sentimentalité banale de son temps sont nécessaires à ses explosions.

Paul Eluard, 'Guillaume Apollinaire', in *Œuvres complètes*, Gallimard, Bibliothèque de la Pléiade, 1968, ii, pp. 895-7. From radio broadcast of 1948.

> ... Et comme il était fatigué
> Il est entré dans un café
> Bonjour bonjour Monsieur Guillaume
> A crié la caissière à tête d'Hermione
> Dites-moi donc le temps qu'il fait
> A l'heure qu'il est
> Et le poète a répondu
> Madame c'est le temps de la Raison ardente
> Il vous faut peindre vos cheveux
> Avec du sperme avec du sang
> Avec le crachat des étoiles
> Et la caissière extasiée a dit c'est un poème

Luc Decaunes, 'Monsieur Guillaume', in *Rimes et Raisons* (Special Apollinaire number), 1946, p. 80.

Il est difficile de dire, en fin de compte—et ce n'est pas là un des aspects les moins attirants de l'énigme qu'il nous propose—si Apollinaire eût pu être ce grand poète auquel il fait songer, ou si ses poèmes, au contraire, avec leur charme équivoque et suggestif, nous donnent de lui une idée avantageuse.

Marcel Raymond, *De Baudelaire au surréalisme*, p. 238.

La plus grande merveille encore, et à beaucoup près, c'est que son *pouvoir d'exaltation*, bien loin de se cantonner dans un passé reculé et aboli, s'exerçait avec la même plénitude dans le présent et tendait de toutes ses forces à anticiper sur l'avenir. Il y a quelque chose d'à jamais bouleversant dans son besoin de cueillir l'émotion que la vie dispense à chaque minute, mais qui nous fuit comme l'eau à laquelle l'enfant fait une coquille de ses mains.

André Breton, 'Ombre non pas serpent mais d'arbre, en fleurs' in *Perspective cavalière*, Gallimard, 1970, pp. 33–4. First published 1954.

... pendant longtemps il a été le phare poétique de notre époque. Il y a quarante ans son rôle de libérateur fut immense. Et l'on peut dire pourtant qu'il régnait. Bien entendu on lui a beaucoup reproché ses défauts, comme si les défauts et les qualités n'étaient pas, comme l'envers et l'endroit d'une étoffe, inséparables sans irréparable dommage pour l'étoffe.

Pierre Reverdy, 'Le Cœur se souvient' in *Cette émotion appelée poésie*, Flammarion, 1974, p. 151. First published 1948.

S'il n'a pas créé de forme poétique personnelle et neuve, c'est qu'il s'en souciait fort peu, qu'il explorait tous les domaines et qu'il a mis dans chacun sa main magistrale, dont l'empreinte ne s'effacera pas. On lui doit d'avoir eu de belles audaces et il ne faut pas lui marchander la louange que, s'il n'était pas venu, un autre que lui ne les eût peut-être pas osées.

Pierre Reverdy, *Nord-Sud, Self Defence et autres écrits sur l'art et la poésie (1917–1926)*, Flammarion, 1975, p. 142. First published 1918.

NOTES

CHAPTER I: KOSTRO

1. A lively debate continues on the subject of Apollinaire's ancestry, which has much of the appeal of a mystery thriller. See the proposals made by Daniel Beauvois in *La Quinzaine littéraire* (No. 208, 16–30 April 1975) and the vigorous response drawn from Michel Décaudin (No. 210, 16–30 May 1975).

2. René Wellek and Austin Warren, *Theory of Literature*, Penguin, 3rd edn, reprinted 1970, p. 80. In the same work, the pseudocriterion of sincerity is also shown in its true colours: 'As for "sincerity" in a poem: the term seems almost meaningless. A sincere expression of what? Of the supposed emotional state out of which it came? Or of the state in which the poem was written? Or a sincere expression of the poem, i.e. the linguistic construct shaping in the author's mind as he writes? Surely it will have to be the last: the poem is a sincere expression of the poem' (p. 208).

CHAPTER II: 'ALCOOLS'

1. For an exegesis reviewing previous attempts, see the edition of *Alcools* by Garnet Rees which is a companion volume to the present work.

2. Cf. Baudelaire, e.g. 'Les Foules' in *Le Spleen de Paris:* 'Le poète jouit de cet incomparable privilège, qu'il peut à sa guise être lui-même et autrui. Comme ces âmes errantes qui cherchent un corps, il entre, quand il veut, dans le personnage de chacun.' Many poets have exploited the notion of 'the double', notably Supervielle.

3. André Bleikasten uses the phrase about Benjy in Faulkner's *The Sound and the Fury* (see *The Most Splendid Failure: A Reading of William Faulkner's The Sound and the Fury*, Bloomington and London: Indiana University Press, 1976). Cf. Beckett's image of 'l'impossible tas' (at the very beginning of *Fin de partie*) symbolising, among other things, a man's life which he can never know in its totality since the heap is complete only when he is dead.

4. The distinction, implied at the start of this chapter, is made by C. Day Lewis in *The Poetic Image*, London: Cape, 1947, p. 116.

5. Cf. Mircea Eliade, *Le Mythe de l'éternel retour*, Paris: Gallimard,

1949. For fire as a various source of fascination for poets, see also Gaston Bachelard, *La Psychanalyse du feu*, Paris: Gallimard, 1949.

CHAPTER III: 'CALLIGRAMMES'

1. André Billy, Preface to Apollinaire, *Œuvres poétiques*, Paris: Gallimard, Bibliothèque de la Pléiade, 1965, p. xliii.

2. Paul Valéry, *Œuvres*, t. ii, Paris: Gallimard, Bibliothèque de la Pléiade, 1962, p. 547.

3. Apollinaire links 'Les Fenêtres' with Delaunay and 'simultanéisme' in *O.C.*, iv, 632, in a letter written in December 1915, by which time he dismisses Delaunay as 'un artiste assez vulgaire'. Consistency was never Apollinaire's strong point.

4. Marie-Jeanne Durry, *Guillaume Apollinaire: Alcools*, t. iii, Paris: Sedes, 1964, p. 233, quoted in Norma Rinsler, 'The War Poems of Apollinaire', *French Studies*, xxv (1971), 169, q.v. for comments by Breton and Aragon and a stimulating discussion of Apollinaire's war poetry.

5. Quoted by John Bayley, 'Slaughter and the real right thing', *Times Literary Supplement* (15 November 1974), p. 1274, col. 1.

6. Alfred de Vigny, *Servitude et grandeur militaires* in *Œuvres complètes*, t. ii, Paris: Gallimard, Bibliothèque de la Pléiade, 1960, p. 531.

CHAPTER V: PROSE AND PLAYS

1. In his classic *Morfologija skazki* (1928) first translated into English in 1958 as *Morphology of the Folk-tale*.

CHAPTER VI: CRITICAL WRITINGS

1. Michel Butor, 'Monument de rien pour Apollinaire' in *Répertoire III*, Paris: Edns de Minuit, 1968, p. 296.

2. André Breton, 'Caractères de l'évolution moderne et ce qui en participe', lecture given in Barcelona, 17 November 1922, reprinted in *Les Pas perdus*, Paris: Gallimard, 1969, p. 151.

3. J.-Cl. Chevalier, 'Apollinaire et la peinture moderne', *Le Français dans le monde*, 40 (April–May 1966), pp. 23–4. For a specific refutation of the comparison with Diderot and Baudelaire, with evidence of Apollinaire's ineptitude and errors, see Francis Steegmuller, *Apollinaire, Poet among the Painters*, New York: Farrar, Strauss, 1963; Harmondsworth: Penguin, 1973, p. 138.

4. Pierre Cabanne, *L'Epopée du cubisme*, Paris: La Table ronde, 1963, p. 50.

5. Norbert Lynton, 'St Apollinaire, tipsy', *The Guardian* (5 November 1968).

6. John Golding, *Cubism: A History and an Analysis, 1907–1914*, London: Faber, 2nd edn reprinted 1971, p. 44. Steegmuller (op. cit., p. 138) captures it nicely: 'For innovation in art Apollinaire had an erratic flair, like that of a hound who picks up too many scents, and he did a good deal of happy, excited barking about it.'

7. Georges Braque, quoted from *The Observer* (1 December 1957) by Steegmuller, op. cit., p. 131.

8. For a wider consideration of the assimilation of content into form in unrhymed poetry, see Roger Little, '*Ut pictura poesis* ...' in *Order and Adventure in Post-Romantic French Poetry*, Oxford: Blackwell, 1973, pp. 244–56.

CHAPTER VII: THE LEGACY

1. The relevant essays with editorial comment may be found in Cyrena N. Pondrom, *The Road from Paris*, Cambridge University Press, 1974. The *comparatiste* will doubtless wish to note the work of a British war poet (i.e. anti-war poet) which has never, to my knowledge, been compared with Apollinaire's. There seems to be no evidence of a direct influence on Robert Nichols, yet his rhyming techniques (half-rhyme, dissonance etc.) and juxtaposition of contrasting registers of language are similar to the French poet's, as may be judged from these extracts from 'The Assault':

> A stream of lead raves
> Over us from the left . . . (We safe under cover!).
> Crash! Reverberation! Crash!
> Acrid smoke billowing. Flash upon flash.
> Black smoke drifting. The German line
> Vanishes in confusion, smoke. Cries, and cry
> Of our men, '*Gah, yer swine!*
> *Ye're for it,*' die
> In a hurricane of shell.
>
> ...
> Go on. Go.
> Deafness. Numbness. The loudening tornado.
> Bullets. Mud. Stumbling and skating.
> My voice's strangled shout:
> '*Steady pace, boys!*'
> The still light: gladness.
> '*Look, sir. Look out!*'
> Ha! ha! Bunched figures waiting.

Revolver levelled quick
Flick! Flick!
Red as blood.
Germans. Germans.
Good! O good!
Cool madness.

I am grateful to Louis Allen, of the University of Durham, for bringing this text to my notice.

2. Pondrom, p. 198.

3. Ibid., pp. 80–1.

4. *The Poetry Review*, I, 8 (August 1912), repr. in Pondrom, see p. 93.

5. 'French Chronicle', *Poetry and Drama* (December 1913), repr. in Pondrom, see pp. 233–5.

6. E. J. H. Greene nips influence-hunting in the bud by declaring in his *T. S. Eliot et la France* (Paris: Boivin, 1951, p. 76): 'pour la beauté du fait, on voudrait qu'Apollinaire eût influé sur le poète anglais, si nombreux sont les parallélismes qu'on pourrait établir! Malheureusement, quand Eliot en vient à lire Apollinaire, vers 1920, celui-ci n'a plus grand'chose à lui apprendre.'

7. Anna Balakian, *André Breton: Magus of Surrealism*, New York: Oxford University Press, 1971, p. 22.

8. For examples and a stimulating discussion, see H. Meschonnic, 'Illuminé au milieu d'ombres', *Europe*, Nos. 451–2 (November–December 1966), p. 162 and passim.

9. The influence of *Les Mamelles de Tirésias* has been limited by the very restricted availability of the text and its virtual disappearance from the stage since its first performance. This restriction should also be borne in mind for other texts such as *L'Enchanteur pourrissant*.

10. André Breton, repr. in *Manifestes du surréalisme*, Paris: Pauvert, 1972, p. 35. For a garland of other definitions of surrealism see C. Abastado, *Introduction au surréalisme*, Paris: Bordas, 1971, p. [5].

11. eugen gomringer, 'from line to constellation', *Image: Kinetic Art: Concrete Poetry*, London: Kingsland Prospect Press, n.d. [1964?], pp. 12–13.

12. From *Spatialisme et poésie concrète*, Paris: Gallimard, 1968, reproduced in C. A. Hackett, *New French Poetry: An Anthology*, Oxford: Blackwell, 1973, pp. 46–7.

CHAPTER VIII: ORDER AND ADVENTURE

1. Cf. 'Order is an equivocal term, as is to a rather lesser degree adventure. Order may be barren, a mere convention, a timid conformity. Adventure may be only a disruptive breaking away. But order

may also be a difficult patterning of a violent movement, the making sense of chaos; and adventure may be the pursuit of the worth-while, the staking of one's all on an activity whose outcome remains unknown, unpredictable.' Ernest Beaumont, 'A Note on *Cinq Grandes Odes*: Some Ambiguities of Order and Adventure', in *Order and Adventure in Post-Romantic French Poetry*, p. 107.

2. Fernand Fleuret, *De Gilles de Rais à Guillaume Apollinaire*, Paris: Mercure de France, 1933, quoted in *Les Critiques de notre temps et Apollinaire*, p. 24.

3. J.-Cl. Chevalier, 'Apollinaire et le calembour', *Europe*, Nos. 451–2 (November–December 1966), p. 70.

4. Quoted by David Garnett in his preface to *The Letters of T. E. Lawrence*, London: Cape, 1938, p. 31.

5. Louis Allen, unpublished note to the author, written in Freetown, Sierra Leone, in late February 1975.

SELECT BIBLIOGRAPHY

The reader is referred for further material and guidance to the analytical bibliography by Claude Tournadre in the very useful compilation
Les Critiques de notre temps et Apollinaire (Garnier, 1971). The list below
concentrates on introductory material and work dealing with
Apollinaire's poetry, particularly *Alcools* and *Calligrammes*.

A. WORKS BY APOLLINAIRE

This volume refers to:

Œuvres complètes (4 vols.), ed. Michel Décaudin, Balland and Lecat,
1965–6. (Abbreviated as *O.C.*)

Œuvres poétiques, ed. P.-M. Adéma and M. Décaudin, Gallimard,
Bibliothèque de la Pléiade, 1956. (Abbreviated as *O.P.*)

Lettres à Lou, Préface de Michel Décaudin, Gallimard, 1969.

Les Peintres cubistes, ed. L. C. Breunig and J.-Cl. Chevalier, Hermann,
1965.

La Fin de Babylone, Bibliothèque des Curieux, 1914.

Les Onze Mille Verges, Cercle du livre précieux, 1963.

Alcools, ed. Garnet Rees, Athlone Press, Athlone French Poets, 1975.

B. CRITICISM ON APOLLINAIRE

(a) Books and special numbers of periodicals:

Pierre-Marcel Adéma, *Guillaume Apollinaire*, La Table ronde, 1968.

Scott Bates, *Guillaume Apollinaire*, New York: Twayne, 1967.

Claude M. Bégué and Pierre Lartigue, *Alcools: Apollinaire*, Hatier, 1972.

LeRoy C. Breunig, *Guillaume Apollinaire*, New York and London:
Columbia University Press, 1969.

J.-Cl. Chevalier, *'Alcools' d'Apollinaire: Essai d'analyse des formes poétiques*,
Minard, 1970.

R. Couffignal, *'Zone' de Guillaume Apollinaire: Structure et confrontations*,
Minard, 1970.

Margaret Davies, *Apollinaire*, Edinburgh and London: Oliver and Boyd,
1964.

Michel Décaudin, *Le Dossier d' 'Alcools'*, Geneva: Droz; Paris: Minard,
nouvelle édition revue 1971. (Abbreviated in text to *Dossier*).

Marie-Jeanne Durry, *Guillaume Apollinaire: 'Alcools'* (3 vols), Sedes,
1956–64.

Europe, Nos. 451–2 (November–December 1966).

Cl. Morhange-Bégué, '*La Chanson du mal-aimé* d'*Apollinaire: Essai d'analyse structurale et stylistique*, Minard, 1970.

Pascal Pia, *Apollinaire par lui-même*, Seuil, 1954 (1969 reprint).

Philippe Renaud, *Lecture d'Apollinaire*, Lausanne: L'Age d'homme, 1969.

Revue des Lettres Modernes, série Guillaume Apollinaire, Nos. 1–13 so far appeared, 1962–1974. (Abbreviated below to *RLM*(GA)).

Francis Steegmuller, *Apollinaire: Poet among the Painters*, New York: Farrar, Strauss, 1963; edn referred to here: Penguin, 1973.

(b) Articles:

LeRoy C. Breunig, 'Apollinaire's "Les Fiançailles" ', *Essays in French Literature* (University of Western Australia), (November 1966).

J.-Cl. Chevalier, 'Apollinaire et le calembour', *Europe*, Nos. 451–2 (November–December 1966).

Michel Décaudin, 'Le Changement de front d'Apollinaire', *Revue des Sciences Humaines*, No. 60 (October–December 1950).

James R. Lawler, 'Music in Apollinaire' in *The Language of French Symbolism*, Princeton University Press, 1969.

S. I. Lockerbie, '*Alcools* et le symbolisme', *RLM*(GA), 2 (1963).

—, 'Le Rôle de l'imagination dans *Calligrammes*', *RLM*(GA), 5, 6 (1966, 1967).

Henri Meschonnic, 'Illuminé au milieu d'ombres', *Europe*, Nos. 451–2 (November–December 1966).

Marc Poupon, 'L'Année allemande d'Apollinaire', *RLM*(GA), 7 (1968).

Norma Rinsler, 'Guillaume Apollinaire's War Poems', *French Studies*, xxv, 2 (April 1971).

SUGGESTIONS FOR FURTHER READING

Roger Shattuck, *The Banquet Years: The Origins of the Avant-garde in France: 1885 to World War I*, New York: Harcourt, Brace; London: Cape, 1961.

Michel Décaudin, *La Crise des valeurs symbolistes*, Toulouse: Privat, 1960.

Marcel Raymond, *De Baudelaire au surréalisme*, Corti, revised edn 1952.

E. Beaumont, J. Cruickshank and J. M. Cocking (eds.), *Order and Adventure in Post-Romantic French Poetry: Essays presented to C. A. Hackett*, Oxford: Blackwell, 1973.

Michael Hamburger, *The Truth of Poetry: Tensions in Modern Poetry from Baudelaire to the 1960s*, Weidenfeld and Nicholson, 1969; edn referred to here: Penguin, 1972.

Kenneth Cornell, *The Post-Symbolist Period: French Poetic Currents 1900–1920*, New Haven: Yale University Press, 1958.

Cyrena N. Pondrom, *The Road from Paris: French Influence on English Poetry 1900–1920*, Cambridge University Press, 1974.

L. Brion-Guerry (ed.), *L'Année 1913* (3 vols.), Klincksieck, 1971–3.

A. J. P. Taylor, *The First World War: An Illustrated History*, Hamish Hamilton, 1963; Penguin, 1966.

Robert Graves, *Goodbye to All That*, Cassell, 1929, 1958; Penguin, 1960.

John Golding, *Cubism: A History and an Analysis 1907–1914*, Faber, 2nd edn 1971.

B. Bowler, *The Word as Image*, Studio Vista, 1970.

R. S. Short and Roger Cardinal, *Surrealism: Permanent Revelation*, Studio Vista, 1970.

INDEX